Finding Your Butkus

The Four Quarters

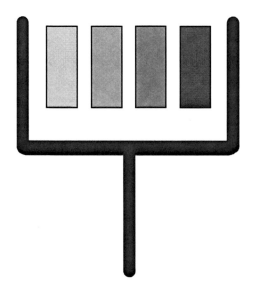

Bob Mueller

First Published in Canada Feb, 2017
by CBK Arts and Entertainment

In partnership with Influence Publishing Inc.

ISBN 978-0-9938086-1-6
ISBN 978-0-9938086-2-3 (Ebook)

For information about booking Bob Mueller for Keynote speaking, corporate or personal training contact:

www.findingyourbutkus.com
www.sportslegendsart.com
bmue51art@gmail.com

A special thanks to Scott Bullard, Ed Comeau and my beautiful wife, Wendy Foster, for their advice and editing skills. An extra shout out to John Graden for pushing me to explore the meaning of my passion.

Praise for Finding Your Butkus

"Admittedly Dick Butkus was a hero for me too. A great read about listening to your inner voice and giving it life."
Steven Pressfield, Legend of Bagger Vance / War of Art

"A good guide to playing better than you did yesterday."
Dick Butkus, HOF '79

"As much as John Lennon was a powerful voice for peace and love in the 60s, Dick Butkus was the smash and crash player in the NFL at the same time. Bob Mueller has done a masterful job of translating the hard-hitting lessons from the legacy of Butkus into smart, practical, and highly effective actionable steps to success that any generation would enjoy and benefit from."
John Graden Executive Director Martial Arts Teachers Association

"Bob Mueller's original work of art packs a similar punch like a withering forearm from the legendary #51 himself. 'Finding Your Butkus' is a metaphor for both business and life that anyone can relate to in terms of what it takes to create a Hall of Fame company or career."
Gair Maxwell, TEC Canada "Speaker of the Year"

"Bob Mueller is an alchemist, turning action into art, football into insight, and philosophy into success. "Finding Your Butkus" is his spellbook for working the magic that makes dreams come true.'
Label Braun, Author *Legends of the Lamed-Vav*

"A fresh look at how to turn your dreams into realities."
Ken Thimmel, Pay it Forward Sports Marketing

"A story with grid iron guts ... persistence meets the Law of Attraction."
Steve Andrich, Cinematographer, NFL Films ESPN

"Butkus played every play with power, intensity and purpose. Bob shows how to live life the same way."
David Rothstein, David Rothstein Music Inc.

"Mueller prompted me to remember that our own journey in life is important and by honoring our selves, we honor our heroes."
Michael Sweeney, Zero to Cruising Captain

"Napoleon Hill (or Brian Tracy) meets football ... Mueller's playbook on life and success captured me instantly with his motivational story-telling style."
Nancy Rose, Washington Children's Choice award for 2016

"Bob has created a masterpiece to maximize Success in all areas of your life. His integrity and true grit and dedication is what makes his advice solid and life changing. Just do what Bob says, you will be so elated you did!"
Colin Sprake, #1 Entrepreneurial Trainer in Canada

"Bob Mueller possesses an extraordinary and diverse skill set. His parallels between Butkus, football and business are brilliant. Bob knows that dedication, determination and commitment are the foundation for self-motivation, leadership and most importantly, being results-driven in career, sports and life. He truly can help find the greatness inside each of us."
Bob Sgarlata, Fortune 500 Executive and Consultant

Dedication

To my mentors, students and friends who live their lives
seeking passion and joy: especially for the departed
"Artists of Life," Jimmy Mac & Steve Sabol.
You meant so much to me.

Acknowledgements

To acknowledge life's meaningful moments is to thank its source. I am literally in the debt of the giants, whose shoulders I have stood upon. The experiences, the joy, and the pain that turned to joy all came from the impact of good people. They are my source, and the moments we shared are my treasure. Beginning at the cradle I received the good fortune of wonderful parents. For Roberta, the totality of your mother's unconditional love has given me the confidence to find my way through every adventure and every relationship.

To the many men and women who have populated my life with their mentorship, friendship and comradery, I owe much. In particular my teachers, Jim Mac Donald, Roy Vollinger and Russ Horsnell – you provided the lessons and the inspiration when I needed it most, making me feel like we were all in it together. For my heroes, from close and from afar, you kept my dreams alive in so many ways. The only way I can repay the debt is to "pay it forward" to those who hear your message through me. I feel like you wrote this book, and I simply copied it down.

From the blessing of a strong and beautiful daughter, Brittany brought an extra joy to a family of men. She, along with my sons, Leigh, Drew and Kieran are my pride. Independent and free, dynamic yet compassionate, and always in my thoughts, I know they are the kind of people that make the world a better place. Our family love is strong.

I was told decades ago that I deserved more from love. I was sent a good woman who saved me, then an offering from the gods brought me a love so deep that no challenge can break it. Wendy, you make me want to be a better man. Your love is kind, your support is so rare it can't be quantified. Thank you, I love you.

To my many students, my extended pride, with so many successes I can scarcely believe that I was a part of your journey, I am grateful for the opportunity to serve. It is to you that I'll leave with the most impactful statement I have ever read.

From the eulogy of my Karate Sensei, Jimmy Mac, a few words he wrote on his death bed: "Thank you to all the men who were fathers to me. Mine was dead and my step dad didn't know how. I won't mention any more names for fear of leaving some off and there have been so many. I love you all. You all made me. Life has been a wonderful gift and experience."

Contents

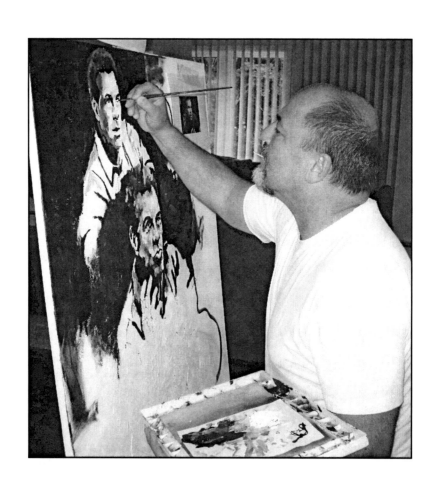

Artist's Statement

As a boy, I began my life as an artist but lost my way with the brush and the canvas, replacing it with the fist of a martial artist. For the next three decades I left the brush, while I made the martial study of body-movement my canvas.

At the age of 47, I again picked up the brush and began to color the canvas with my life's lessons. A Karate-do Sensei's intense study of expansion, contraction and power of how to move became the basis for my art. Movement was my life and now it is my art.

Every athlete, sport or team has a unique set of motions and colors that becomes their signature. These distinctive qualities create a whole portrait of the subject.

My objective is to capture the mood and personality of the athlete through the bold colors and body dynamics of their sport. There is nothing static in sport and competition, thus, I combine the realism of the subject with the surrealism of the movement.

The colors combine strokes of palette knife and brush with layers of medium to create the movement in the work. I want the viewer to feel his struggle to succeed and the will to win in the piece. My work, like my life, is the love of the underdog, overcoming the odds and succeeding to rise above the ordinary.

I choose the athlete as my medium of expression because I know their struggle of private self-doubt and of public bravo.

It represents the human experience.

It fascinates me.

Bob Mueller

Foreword

Bob Mueller came into my life the way I imagine he enters a lot of lives. First, the old karate master knocked gently. Then he kicked the door down.

He'd sent a letter to my boss Steve Sabol. Steve, the late, legendary president of NFL Films, had many wonderful qualities. One of them was always taking the time to read and respond to fan letters. Bob had written Steve a letter about his lifelong admiration for Steve and his work, and to tell his own unique story. Another of Steve's best qualities was the impeccable ability to recognize a good story when he saw one. Steve read the letter and passed it on to me. "Call this guy and see if there's anything there," he said. This was early 2007. Seven years later, I can report with certainty that yes, something is definitely there.

I called Bob. We talked for a while. Well, he talked for a while. I listened and smiled. I called back a few weeks later to tell him we wanted to come to British Columbia to film his story. At this point in the production process we usually get down to the details with the subject, try to pin down what to shoot and when ... all the logistics. I didn't have to do a lot of work on this one. Bob already had the whole three-day shoot mapped out.

A year later, ""Finding Your Butkus"," a thirteen minute feature about Bob's life won an Emmy. It remains one of the works I am most proud of, the story of an irrepressible spirit who lives his life with passion and commitment—the story, in other words, of an artist.

Bob and I have remained friends through the ensuing years. Two of his paintings hang in my office, including one depicting my favorite athlete of all time, Mario Lemieux. It hangs right above the computer where I edit, serving as a dual inspiration.

When I look at Lemieux I see excellence in its purest form, effortless and angular and elegant. When I look at Bob's craftsmanship I am reminded there is no such thing as effortless excellence. Lemieux's was a beautiful illusion.

The reality of excellence and of art is the work poured into it, the sweat and effort and struggle that make it appear like it was always that way.

I am grateful to have met Bob, and to call him my friend. His pursuit of his passions is an ongoing inspiration to me, and I look forward to the many joys his life will bring us in the months and years to come.

Keith Cossrow
Coordinating Producer
NFL Films
May, 2014

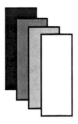

Introduction

Have you ever had a feeling that became a thought, then, the thought became an obsession? Ever fallen in love, done something on a whim or followed your gut?

Are you a fan of something or somebody? What if? What would you do, who would you meet, where would you go, if you knew you could not fail?

In 1937 Napoleon Hill wrote, "Thoughts are things, powerful things, when mixed with definiteness of purpose, persistence, and a burning desire; translate into riches and other material objects." Combine that thought with the old adage; "The person thinking about something is usually passed by someone doing something" and you'll begin to find your Butkus – your true passion in life.

I had done something and now, almost by accident, I was in the middle of a whirlwind. The dream-like funnel dropped me in the corner office at One NFL Way, Mt. Laurel, New Jersey - it was NFL Films.

"Is this real? Why am I here?"

"Is that who I think it is?"

"Is that what I think it is?"

Surely I would wake up from this dream soon. I had to! This couldn't really be happening, but it was.

The corner office was Steve Sabol's, the NFL legend. And no, it wasn't a dream. We were arm and arm as his staff took the picture of us holding a golden EMMY Award.

Years before, many decades actually, I had been a football loving kid in British Columbia, Canada. I loved playing football and watching the NFL on TV, especially the highlight films. That's where I first heard the voice and felt the presence of Steve Sabol. His films stirred my imagination. I loved the poetic slow motion images, thundering music and captivating story lines. As a fan, everything about NFL Films was bigger than life.

Being a fan of something is one thing, but how on earth did I get here in this office with this man? Luck perhaps, heaven sent for certain, but it sure as hell wasn't by accident!

The year before, my fortunes had changed during a moment of frustration. I had written a letter on a whim, then had a paralyzing pause and didn't send it. In my life I have rarely vacillated on anything, yet I sat on this letter for a week debating the pros and cons of sending it. Then one day I read a familiar statement again: "When you have a good idea - do it immediately!" I went to the post office and promptly mailed my letter.

A few weeks later a post card showed up with a Bruno Nagurski stamp on it from NFL Films. The white 5 x 7 card had the NFL Films logo and a hand-written note:

BOB – THANKS FOR THE DVD AND YOUR KIND WORDS ABOUT NFL FILMS!
IF WE HAVE ANOTHER TV SPECIAL ON DICK BUTKUS, AND ONE IS IN THE PLANNING STAGES RIGHT NOW, WE WILL DEFINITELY INCLUDE YOUR WORK AND YOUR STORY.
BEST STEVE

Eleven months later, almost to the day, ""Finding Your Butkus"" won the 2008 Emmy Award for 'Outstanding Long Feature.' With only desire and self-belief I had unconsciously followed Hill's teachings, "Thoughts are things,"- powerful things that are realized through action.

Dreams do come true, even crazy ones! ""Finding Your Butkus"" isn't just an Emmy winning story, it's a true story. An everyman yarn that tells how to make your thoughts and dreams become reality. Dreams so real that it will wake you in the middle of the night to take action.

I'll show you the exact strategies and life lessons that took me from the Canadian prairies, crisscrossing the continent to become a martial arts entrepreneur, an Emmy winning artist and best selling author. How just being present with my dreams attracted business opportunities and created friendships, particularly with the late, great, Steve Sabol.

What you will learn is a unique mixture of martial arts philosophies and self-help tools for realizing your own potential and why what you already know, right now, is the key to unlocking your dreams and desires. Here are "The Four Quarters" and my life long journey to live without limitations and find my unstoppable self.

The Hero Within?

The Japanese have a saying: "On Ko Chi Shin" which means "By asking old things, know new things" - Richard Kim.

Many times we hear words, sayings, and expressions without giving them much thought. Classic sayings like: "Going or giving it the whole nine yards," "A rule of thumb," or having to "Bite the bullet" are common everyday sayings. We knowingly apply them to our everyday conversations without much thought. Although we may know the context of what we are saying and how to use it in a conversation, do we really know the meaning?

For instance "Biting the bullet" is to accept something difficult or unpleasant. Typically the meaning is extended to do something willingly, regardless of the discomfort and do it, with a certain amount of grace. History states; during emergency battlefield surgery, if there was no time for painkillers or anesthesia, the surgeon offered a bullet. Patients were told to bite down on a bullet in an attempt to distract them from the pain.

I suppose we have all seen enough westerns to guess the meaning of that one. But, how about something a little more obscure?

Do you know the meaning of "To give it or go for the whole nine yards?" Ah, another easy one! Meaning: "to try one's best," something you might think comes from a football or sports analogy. Would you believe this is a saying from World War II? Fighter pilots, readying for combat, received a 9-yard chain of ammunition. Therefore, when a gunner used all of his ammunition on one target, he was said to "Give it the whole 9 yards!"

Again, not knowing the origin of a saying is usually fine as long as you know how to use it but there are always exceptions to everything, particularly rules.

Have you ever used the term, "The rule of thumb?" This is a common expression and yes, measurements are important. Thus, invoking a general rule of thumb should be a good benchmark to getting things right.

However, what if the mark is based on a 17th century legend? One where an English Judge, Francis Buller, ruled it permissible for a husband to beat his wife with a stick, given that the stick was no wider than his thumb!

Political correctness is important these days, but even if it wasn't, you probably won't want to be labeled with that one. At least not as a rule of thumb!

I hope all this doesn't "Rub you the wrong way." It's just my way to "break the ice" about heroes, their meanings and importance in our lives. Whether you like the idea of having a hero or not, societies since the beginning of time have always admired exceptional behavior. Persons who did more, achieved some greatness, or put another's needs before their own are deemed to be heroic.

Webster's dictionary defines the hero as "Being a person, typically a man, who is admired or idealized for courage, outstanding achievements, or noble qualities." On the other hand, a large sandwich stuffed with meats and cheese is also known as a "Hero." While the sandwich may be tasty, it is not particularly admired, nor is it noble!

For me, defining the term hero has only one specific role. It's a role that fires our imagination and fills us with desire. Has there ever been a child born who did not openly dream of heroic acts or pretend to be a hero of some type? Even in your silence, do you not dream of things like winning a lottery or creating some great success? What if you had a big windfall of some sort? What would your dreams have you do? My best guess is you would want to give to your family, perhaps help a friend, or donate to a cause you believe in. If that's correct, ask yourself why? Why would you want to share your success?

The heroic answer comes from the historian, Joseph Campbell. He says, "We all, in some way, are heroes and we are living myth. But do you listen to the call?"

Campbell, a 20th century philosopher, wrote and lectured extensively about mythology. His monomyth of life speaks to the hero's rites of passage. In his book, "Hero with a Thousand Faces," he talks about mythology and the journey of the hero. Summarized, he states, "A hero ventures forth from the world of common day, into a region of supernatural wonder. Fabulous forces are there encountered and a decisive victory is won. The hero comes back from this mysterious adventure with the power to bestow boons on his fellow man."

A heroic journey, if you look closely, appears in all our lives. Wanting to be noticed, be it however subtle, is your first heroic act. It calls you to take a journey and launches you into each of life's adventures. Everyone's voyage may be different, but each journey has similar steps, comparable meanings, and expected outcomes.

Every hero starts out as an ordinary person and receives a call to enter an unusual world. If he accepts the call, he must face tasks and trials that lead to many intense and severe challenges. If he survives, he may achieve a great gift (the goal or "boon") which typically is the discovery of self-important knowledge. Now, armed with this special knowledge, he must decide whether to return to the ordinary world. The return is also fraught with trials and tribulations. If overcome, he receives a "hero's welcome" and then shares his gift to improve the world.

While we recognize it in others, seeing our own heroic journey often goes unnoticed, particularly by ourselves. We tend to reserve the name of hero for only the bravest or most exceptional among us. Yet Campbell argues that simply being born, going from the water and safety of the womb, to the elements of air and the dangers of birth, is in itself, a heroic journey. Certainly our mothers, giving birth, are heroes who knowingly face the pain of delivery and accept the fear of the unknown.

If Campbell is correct, each person is granted a mythic, god-like journey and the potential to be a hero. In the bible, Jesus asks, "Do you see what you see? Do you hear what you hear?" When opportunity knocks at the door, do you answer the call? Do you see what you see?

Yes, realizing your own potential is the true challenge - a challenge that is often lost in the minutia of life. I suspect that, should heaven be true, what flashes through your mind just before your death are the moments in your life that felt like they vibrated with the Gods.

In Steven Pressfield's book, "The War of Art," he examines the entropy of resistance for artists and warriors alike. When I read his dream story named "Largo," he touched my heart. Largo spoke to me profoundly, as the writer summed up in a few short paragraphs the essence of what Joseph Campbell is teaching.

Pressfield writes, "One night I had this dream. I was part

of the crew of an aircraft carrier. Only the ship was stuck on dry land. It was still launching its jets and doing its thing, but it was marooned a half a mile from the ocean.

The sailors all knew how screwed up the situation was. They felt it as a keen and constant distress. The only bright spot was there was a Marine gunnery sergeant on board nicknamed "Largo." In the dream it seemed like the coolest name anyone could possibly have. Largo. I loved it. Largo was one of those hard-core senior noncoms like the Burt Lancaster character, Warden, in "From Here to Eternity."

The one guy on the ship who knows exactly what is going on, the tough old Sarge who makes all the decisions and actually runs the show. But where was Largo? I was standing miserably by the rail when the captain came over and started talking to me. Even he was lost. It was his ship, but he didn't know how to get it off dry land. I was nervous, finding myself with the brass, and couldn't think of a thing to say.

The skipper didn't seem to notice; he just turned to me casually and said, "What the hell are we gonna do, Largo?"

Like Largo, ""Finding Your Butkus"" involves this same innate discovery. Using Campbell's theory, I looked at Dick Butkus to see if and how he fits.

Butkus left the ordinary world, answering the call to an extraordinary world: the NFL and the Chicago Bears. The trials and tasks of his journey caused him severe challenges. He played at the highest level, with reckless abandon, on destroyed and damaged knees. He endured a career playing on a losing team, where in spite of his extraordinary abilities and determination, he never won anything of any significance. Even so, his efforts were mythologized, and when he returned to the ordinary world, he became a legend.

The Butkus legend spurred my own heroic journey of 40

years. Beginning as a teenager, I created art about a legendary hero. I left the comfort of my talent for a life journey filled with ups, downs and misdirection. Then starting over, I renewed the adventure, and created my own mythic journey of skyrocketing successes, disappointments, realizations, and most certainly, redemption. When I returned to my forfeited youthful fantasies, my talent led me to find the hero of my dreams and create a mythic story around it.

John Ruskin, a nineteenth century artist and prominent social thinker wrote, "The highest reward for a person's toil is not what they get for it, but what they become."

Mythology exists to give us the road map and what you become is the mythic pot of gold at the end of the rainbow. Stories and myths created by another's journey are meant to inspire action and to show us the way. But, the hero's job is not to impress, rather it is to give us both the knowledge and the confidence to do it for ourselves.

Sensei/Philosopher Richard Kim, known as a 20th Century Samurai, teaches, "Knowledge you can pass on —wisdom, you must get your own."

Finding your true passion is not an outcome. It's a process of self-discovery. Knowing the meaning of what you say, and taking the action to live up to your own potential, is to find the hero within.

Once realized, you will never be able to deny yourself again.

Take-away

Know the meaning of words – particularly your words.   Your story has value and you are valuable.

Everyone is born to have their own heroic life. Everyone has opportunities to succeed. But, when opportunity knocks, do you answer the door?

You are the hero you are seeking and you will discover your true power when you learn to tell your story.

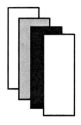

The Field of Play

Before we get too excited about playing, learning our playbook, and scoring touchdowns, we need to look at the field of play. If you wanted to learn how to drive a car or sail a boat you'd want to know something about the roads or the ocean. Like any environment, understanding the rules, dimensions and topography is essential to success.

Some aspects of the field of play are immutable "Laws of the Nature", while others are simple rules that can assist you to play well. If it's a law, like the field is 100 yards long, it cannot be broken. To underscore the significance of our field of play, the football field is an exacting arena called a "Gridiron". The terrain is clearly marked and no amount of wishing, whining or scheming can change this fact.   In truth, every element of the field is governed by law of measurement and is unchallengeable.

It was Benjamin Franklin who first lamented a universal truth,   "Our new Constitution is now established, and has an appearance that promises permanency; but in this world nothing can be said to be certain, except death and taxes."

What isn't permanent, are the rules that regulate the field. This is where the play portion becomes part of the field and makes anything possible. While you cannot change a law, you can adapt every part of the field as it pertains to how you play on it. Expanding the idea of playing on the field is to understand what you bring to world. There are six billion people inhabiting a planet that is governed by natural laws, creating a collective consciousness that you are but a spec of. Add to that the concept of time, and you become an insignificant spec here for a millisecond and then returned to dust. On that happy note, as insignificant as you may be, you somehow have the ability to harness the power of the universe with your thoughts and desires. More plainly put: what you bring to the field of play matters. You matter, and you can make a difference.

Webster defines the field of play as "the part of the field that is officially marked as a place where the action happens: the playing field. Spectators are not allowed on the field".

There it is. This simple statement, over rides all the flowery words and universal platitudes ever spoken: a place where the action happens, spectators not allowed! The game of life is the same as the field of play.

*Highlighted boxes in the book are referenced as "Mueller Law" or more appropriately named "Bob B.S." – Bob's Belief Systems!

> **Bob's B.S.**
> If you want to be successful you can't do it from the sidelines. You must go where the action is.

Let's take the field and go onto the Gridiron. While there are far too many details to know about the game of football we do need to understand the basic lay of the land. Let's keep it simple. The basic dimensions of the football field are 100 yards long and 53.33 yards wide. Parallel lines, 5 yards apart, run from the sides of the field with each yard marked off individually down the center. These are called the hash-marks. There is a goal line at either end of the field along with a set of goal posts. Each goalpost has a center base post with a cross bar spanning 18.6 feet wide and two uprights reaching to a total height of 30 feet. Coincidentally, when a touchdown is scored, the referee holds both arms straight up signaling the score and looking every bit like a goal post.

The gridiron is a set field where every play can be measured exactly. This allows each play to become "a game of inches" and this where things start to get interesting. Along with the set gridiron lines, we now add a moveable line. The "line of scrimmage" is like an old-fashioned slide ruler that moves with each calculation. This arbitrary line could be called the universal challenge line, as this is where the action is. The football is placed on the line of scrimmage with opposing teams facing each other on either side of the line. The challenge is for your team to move the ball in the direction of the opponent's goal line and score a touchdown.

Unlike most other sports, like soccer, hockey or rugby, where the play is constant, a football play has a beginning and an end. It takes only a few seconds to complete and each play results in either going forward or going backward. At the end of each play the line of scrimmage is reset and a new challenge is set. There in lies the magic. With every gain or loss a new set of circumstances are put in play and everyone has to adjust their plans to accommodate the new reality!

There is an endless amount of information about an actual football game and how it is played, but that is not the purpose of this book. Finding Your Butkus uses the game of football as a metaphor of how the game of life is played. How your individual success, as part of the bigger picture of life, is measured against everything you do.

To that end, you are on a life field that has both a beginning and an end. The line of scrimmage is constantly moving either for you or against you. The playing field is the only part of the game that is fair and true. Everything else on the field of play is competition, chance and circumstance. What's fascinating is this is the ultimate team game, where every player on the field must co-ordinate with every other player to succeed. To do that, each player must first win an all out individual battle against the opponent in front of them, then, add their success or failure to the team effort. The resulting combined team effort causes the line of scrimmage to either advance or retreat.

Life is a team sport that creates winning ways only when everyone plays full out. To be able to run effective plays in life and business you must first understand the game you are playing, then accept your role and finally maximize your own particular contribution or play. You could say that your life's scrimmage line is set every morning when you get up. The field is there, waiting for you to get in action.

Bob's B.S.
When you put your hand in the dirt (field),
you put everything on the line!

Simply putting yourself on the line is to be a warrior. Win or lose, live or die, it all happens in the course of the play. You can't score the touchdowns you need from the sidelines. Winning in the game of life is won in the trenches of determination and desire. It's a game of inches, a game where consistent effort gets you into the touchdown zone. Your own personal line of scrimmage is forever moving and continually measured by the gridiron. Success on life's field of play happens when you play full out!

Take-away

The field of play is where the action is,
no spectators allowed.
The line of scrimmage is a universal challenge line
that moves with every play.
To succeed you must play full out.

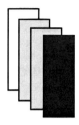

The Playbook

""Finding Your Butkus"," like a football game is divided into two halves. In the first half you'll be issued the playbook. Inside are six stories, like the six points you receive when you score a touch down. They contain the basic elements you will need to formulate your own playbook and create the success you are looking for. Planning and preparation are the keys to recognizing opportunities when they appear.

President Dwight D. Eisenhower once said, "In preparing for battle I have always found that plans are useless, but planning is indispensable." In other words expect the unexpected. If you build your abilities and train yourself to expect success, you'll be able to deal with unforeseen issues and challenges.

Perhaps your challenge right now is that you don't know anything about, or god forbid, don't care about the game of football! Forget for a moment that football is about freakishly fast, massive men crashing into each other with wild abandon. Instead, think of a chess game, where you analyze all your players, looking at their strengths and weaknesses to develop plans of how to best succeed.

Rather than Pawns and Rooks, your players will have names like Quarterback, Halfback, and Linebacker. Every player has a role in every play, and while the ultimate goal is to score a win, each play is designed to also teach. Every play, be it successful or not, guides the team and teaches the players. The players who learn from their experience ultimately develop better plays and achieve greater success.

A football playbook, like those used by NFL teams, can be the size of an old fashioned telephone book, only more complicated. With that in mind I have chosen just six plays for my playbook and they are the basis for my winning life strategies.

In this day and age of computer science and unlimited data you might ask, "Why only six plays? Isn't that a little light?"

No, absolutely not! Vince Lombardi, arguably the most famous coach of all time, had one key play. He had the Packer Sweep, a football play that had been around since the beginning of time. Well at least since the frozen tundra! Lombardi theorized: if he could run just one play with absolute perfection, he could create a mental attitude about winning. He said, "Gentlemen, we will chase perfection, and we will chase it relentlessly, knowing all the while we can never attain it. But along the way, we shall catch excellence."

Starting in 1959, with the worst team in football, Lombardi caught excellence, winning five NFL Championships in nine years. That record has never been matched.

Our six plays are: "The Dive, The Sweep, The Draw-Option, The Texas Option, The Reverse, and The Bomb!" These are all contained in the first half of the book. Each play has a story, a lesson, and a life strategy guaranteed to inspire action. I expect you to gain a lot of personal ground and score many life touchdowns. But of course, the real goal is for you to create your own "take-aways!"

Then the second half is a whole new game!

As my own football coach, Roy Vollinger, liked to say at half time, "Boys, the score is zero to zero. It's a new start. It's a whole new game! Let's win!"

Once you have the playbook and understand your own formations, you'll select which plays are best for you. Whether you choose, like Lombardi, just one, or you use all six, you'll be ready to play the whole game – "The Four Quarters!"

"The Four Quarters" is my true story of ""Finding Your Butkus"." I'll take you right from raw desires, to the full circle reality checks and beyond. Learning life lessons, good or bad, are the building blocks of your future success. As Anthony Robbins says, "When you succeed, you party. When you fail, you ponder." Both have value and both are necessary.

There is an ebb and flow to every game and every life. It's the motion of emotion that either carries you forward or paralyzes you into submission.

Bob's B.S.
Everything that can happen, will happen!
Don't quit.
Learn to be resilient, as you will need to survive to thrive.
Losing is a part of winning.
To succeed you must play full out.

The old judo saying is true; "Fall down seven times - get up eight."

Bob's B.S.
Accept you will be knocked down,
but refuse to stay there.

Remember, it's not what you did; it's what you do next that counts. It's what you do on each play. And what you learn is what builds your abilities to find a way to win The Game – quarter by quarter.

The first quarter is about preparing, how you start, and how it began for me, thus it's "the kickoff." The second quarter, "the game plan," is your strategy and learning about the competition. The third quarter, the "ball control," is often tumultuous and based on momentum and circumstance. Again, it's not what happens to you in the game; it's how you deal with it. Finally the fourth quarter, the outcome, is all about late game heroics, thus it is the "4th quarter comeback!"

Yes, life is a game, and every quarter is important. Returning to my football explanation. What if you viewed your life as a series of plays where you would win or lose? Each play must be learned from. If you accept the lessons that both success and failure brings, you will ultimately win the game. My first half stories are the lessons.

In the second half, all the elements of the 2008 Emmy winning story ""Finding Your Butkus"" are told in "The Four Quarters." This is about how to win the game - how I won the game of life- one quarter at a time!

Are you ready? Let's "Play ball!"

Take-away

Plans are are useless, planning is indispensable.
Accept that you will knocked down, but refuse to stay there.

THE PLAYBOOK

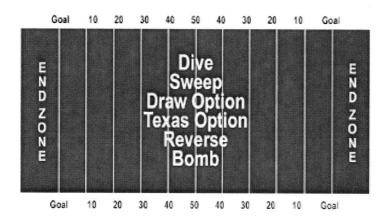

THE LIFE GAME

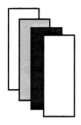

Que Sera, Sera

Play#1 The Reverse

My inclination is to begin with some basic power plays, so you can build your playbook from the bottom to the top. In fact that's exactly where I started when I first formulated this concept. I figured I'd build a foundation by starting with basic plays like the "Dive" and the "Sweep" - plays that can move you forward and build confidence. However, after laying out the foundation, I remembered Robert Fulgum's statement, "All I ever needed to know, I learned in kindergarten."

What if, as a child, while you were learning the basic plays of life - look both ways, play fair, and don't take things that aren't yours, you also were told things that weren't true? Is that possible? What I learned during my kindergarten confused me, creating an inner conflict that still seeks a reckoning to this day.

Perhaps this has a familiar ring to it. What if one of your first life-plays you learned was the "Reverse?" The reverse is a basic play of deception. Twenty-five hundred years ago, in 450 AD, the famous Chinese general, Sun Tzu, taught, "All warfare is based on deception. Hence, when able to attack, we must seem unable."

The reverse play in football has the quarterback pitch the football to the halfback who, running to the outside, seeks to

29

make an end sweep around the opponents and create a break away run. At the last minute, with the defenders in hot pursuit and seemingly unable to advance, the halfback hands the ball to another player running in the opposite or reverse direction. Done well, the reverse fools and demoralizes! This play steals confidence and makes the defense question their basic instincts. The defensive objective during the confusion is to hold their ground and not be fooled by the mis-direction. They must trust what they know and not over react.

In the game of life you must learn to play both ways - both offence and defense, always holding to your core beliefs. The reverse play, as it happens in life, usually tends to come from acts of "friendly fire." People, particularly ones close to you, may try to get you to reverse your opinion looking for ways to control you. Don't be fooled. Stand your ground. Don't be reversed.

"When I was just a little girl, I asked my mother, what will I be," sang Doris Day, "Will I be pretty? Will I be rich? Here's what she said to me - Que Sera, sera – Whatever will be will be. The future's not ours to see, Que Sera, sera."

In the year I was born, this "it is what it is" composition spent 15 weeks on Billboard's Top 10 charts, eventually winning the 1956 Oscar Award for best song.

My earliest memory, be it remembered or simply retold, is of my first day of kindergarten. As a precocious four year old, I walked five blocks to school all by myself. To be sure, parental supervision was different in the 1950's, with more freedom and less hazards for kids, but even then, seeing a confident little guy walking alone was a bit unusual.

The joy of "I can do it myself" was complimented by a deep emotional need for praise and the desire to please my parents. My walk was the first unknown journey of my life. A pattern I would repeat over and over, taking a chance to please someone else, while giving them the power – my power. This particular power was first given to my father.

Later, as a nine year old, I fancied myself to be an artist, a creative writer, and a collector. My subject matter was Superheroes - the kind you find in comic books. I chose "Marvel Comics," "The Amazing Spiderman," "Thor the Thunder God" and "The Fantastic Four" as my mentors. Each month I eagerly awaited the latest editions to arrive at the local drug store. Writer Stan Lee, created intimate stories that spoke to me, while Jack Kirby and Steve Ditko's artwork hypnotized my imagination and fueled my growing talent. I loved how the characters day-dreamed internally, then transformed to be their own superhero, complete with costumes to wear and bad guys to overcome! What kid doesn't want to have a mask and run around with a cape flowing freely behind them?

I especially loved the magazine covers and as a comic book collector, at twelve cents apiece, I reveled with each new purchase. A memorable acquisition was the 1968 cover of a new character, "The Invincible Ironman," #1 of 1 May, a first edition. Even at nine years old, I understood the significant value of having something original.

My heroes taught me how to copy and draw. They developed my eye for detail and impressed my formative mind with bold color and vivid composition. These characters inspired me to dream, and they allowed me to be a dreamer. As time is relative, especially to a young mind, it is hard to know whether the time spent here was just a few fascinating months, or perhaps many years of cosmic yearning. All I am sure of is that I read, I drew, and I loved my superhero dreams.

"Que, sera, sera" is a childhood song with a sweet message. Unfortunately, few of us escape our childhoods with our dreams intact. Children are impressionable and vulnerable and, almost always, completely open. "What will be, will be" is more often your will being bent and shaped with and without your permission.

One day after school, new comic book in hand, I rushed home so I might read the latest edition before supper. As I entered my bedroom, I focused on an empty drawer, immediately knowing my superhero sanctuary had been violated. Gone! My collection, all my treasures, were gone - thrown out, as if they were garbage! My father didn't like dreamers, as they provided little value to him in his military life. He saw the deed as his right to enforce his will, wanting to make his values be mine. My daydreams had not pleased him, and now my tears and anger only reinforced the belief that his actions were just and correct. He considered it his duty to show me what was important in life, so he threw out my treasures and my art, as his way of saving me from myself.

That moment created a conflict between the dreamer who wanted to be desired, and the boy who needed to please. The pleaser in me continued to seek my father's approval, but the dreamer began a life of quiet and, sometimes not so quiet, rebellion. While it would take decades to recall the feeling of that day and cry again about its loss, a deep anger of unresolved pain divided my devotions.

Rebellion is always about control and oppression. Submission always carries resentment, or as the renowned speaker, Brian Tracy, says, "A man changed against his will, - is of the same opinion ... still!" As a child, I quickly let go of my initial anger, forgot about it, and then stuffed the event away, finding alternative ways to fuel my dreams.

Let me ask you a question. What did you want to be when you grew up? Perhaps you have heard this riddle; "Sticks & stones will break your bones, but, (say it with me) …. words will never hurt me."

As a kid, I was a dreamer - adoring art, writing and loving my comic Superheroes. When my father threw my comic books away he told me that artists & dreamers didn't make it in life. He sought control; well intended or not, he tried to take what he did not own - my dreams. What he couldn't take was my talent and my drive to succeed, but he did create a nagging doubt. Destructive seeds of discontent eroded the belief that my talent had value and without value, I voluntarily let go of my childish dreams, trading them for alternative, more useful skills.

I suspect broken bones would have taken a few months to heal, but painful words take time. For many years I fed the wolf of avoidance and the guilt of a hidden hurt. After grade eleven I quit school, quit art, and quit football. I avoided anything to do with art. Instead, I replaced my creative talents, reversing my focus with the ethics of labor and hard work. While that time was not wasted, it was not what I wanted. My dual career as a builder and a martial arts expert taught me to move through life with both confidence and competence. I traded dreams for skills, and focused my natural born ambition to one of doing, rather than being. I found success by being the best I could be, promoting other peoples' dreams and by pleasing them. While it gave me pleasure, it did not give me what I desired. It made me restless.

Do you know that only 9% of people are doing what they dreamed of as a kid? And, 91% of our population is eventually unhappy with what they do, and what they have become! Of the lucky 9%, only 1% of these happy people enjoy the success they dreamed of. My work over the years has put me in the position to hear others' fears and their dreams. So many people have childhood terrors and horrific recollections of abuse, lack and hardship – far worse than losing comic books. Our internal predator preys on these memories and embellishes the stories we feed ourselves.

We all have limiting beliefs and unfulfilled ambitions. Limits that trace their roots to the events of our childhood, when our unguarded minds were open and absorbed every detail, be it good or bad. Is there an event in your childhood that you have suppressed? Something stuffed deep inside that has blocked you in some way from achieving what you want? Never mind achieving, many people don't feel worthy enough to even look. Do you know your story?

Have you ever been reversed? Like the analogy of crabs in a barrel - when one crab tries to climb out, all the other crabs cling to the one seeking freedom, pulling them back down into the barrel. Perhaps the crabs are saying, "Stay safe! Stay with us! – It might not be great here, but a least we know what it is."

Have you ever had well-meaning people, usually family or the ones closest to you, tell you not to follow your dreams? Or worse, they try to reverse you and your thoughts, demanding that you take on their opinion. Like the crabs, when you reach to raise yourself up to a new level, you feel the force of others seeking to keep you where you are. "Stay safe. Listen to us. We know what is best for you, because it is best for us."

The question to ask yourself when you are being reversed is, "Whose life was I born to live? Theirs or mine?" The solution lies not in the opinions and fears of others, but rather in discovering your own true value, and your own story.

More importantly, do you know what your story means? Our stories have made us what we are today. Nine percent? Or ninety one percent? Que Sera, sera.

The fact is, it's not what happened to you – it's what you make it mean. The most crushing blow can also be a rally point that empowers your future success. Similarly, the most innocent slight may shatter your confidence and hold you back. The choice is yours.

Remember who you are, and make it mean something that serves you. What you do today, what will be is up to me. Que Sera, sera.

The two circles of reality

This is what hapenned to you

This is what you made it mean

What are you telling yourself?

My superheroes never left. They simply slept for a time, waiting for me to wake up. Once I collected the necessary tools to understand their value and allowed them to return, I did so with an internal wisdom. Their resurrection had only one purpose: to please me - no one else.

The lyrics, "What ever will be will be" have been forever amended to "Que Sera, sera, what will be – is up to me!"

Take-away

Discover or remember your story.
Where is your beginning? Find the significant event, your earliest memory, and start your story there.
Create a philosophy around the story that explains, for you, what the story represents.
If needed, re-frame the story to make it a positive, life-affirming, empowering event.
Defend against the reverse – don't be fooled.
Own your story!
Make it mean what you need it to mean.
If it's to be - it's up to me.

What's a Butkus?

Play #2 The Dive Play

Now that you have a solid defense protecting you from the reverse, let's look to gain some positive ground. The Dive Play is the most basic play in the game. The objective: Gain One Yard. The quarterback takes the snap, pivots, and hands the football to the fullback - who slams, head on, into the scrimmage line. The goal is to gain a yard or two. It's not pretty, and it rarely creates a big play, but it builds confidence by creating a clear objective - then accomplishing it. Simply put, if you don't have the drive and determination to gain one yard, how in the world could you expect to score a big touchdown?

Jerry Kramer, the renowned Offensive Guard of the 1960's Green Bay Packers, tells the back-story behind his coach, Vince Lombardi, and the most famous block in NFL History. It happened with just 19 seconds left in the 1967 Championship, a game that became known as the "Ice Bowl." The Packer's offense was on the goal line, just one yard away from scoring the potential winning touchdown. Lombardi called the same play, the Dive play, three times in a row and they failed the first two times. You see, the temperatures that day were a record -37 degrees below zero. With the field a sheet of ice, footing was bad and by the end of the game it was a simple contest of wills.

During the time out, just before the final play, Lombardi weighed his options deciding, "Run it again." Looking at Kramer he added, "If you can't gain a yard – you don't deserve to be a champion!"

Subsequently Kramer blew his man off the line and quarterback Bart Starr, keeping the ball, ran behind his block and scored with the Dive Play. With decisive determination they found the most basic way to win. Instead of searching the outer limits of his team's abilities, Lombardy had his men look inward. Find your power within yourself! Do it now and do it well!

Finding something assumes that you are looking for it! ""Finding Your Butkus"," at its core, means to find something that you already possess. It is already part of you, perhaps hidden deep inside your psyche or more likely, simply hiding in plain site. Right below your nose, in your heart.

In Kevin Costner's movie, "A Field of Dreams," his character, Ray Kinsella, hears a voice from the cornfield, "If you build it, he will come." He is asked to trust a whisper and hear a feeling. The voice wants him to listen and then take action - completely on faith.

While the tall corn may not be calling you, I'm certain you have had an inspired thought while showering or driving a car. A gut feeling that says - take action.

Your Butkus, I say with a wink, is found slightly south by reaching around and finding your rear end. With both hands, I might add! Perhaps the reason you haven't found your Butkus as yet is because you're sitting on it!

So, what is a Butkus?

No, it's not But-Kis, its pronounced But-Kus. You say it deliberately, and always with attitude. If you are a sports fan you have probably heard the name, Dick Butkus. In fact most people in North America have heard that name, although they may not know who or what it is.

And yes, it is an odd name.

Years ago, a child I was teaching asked me what my assistant's name was. The little guy was part of a group of four and five year old karate tots. Although Spencer was the smallest in the class, he had one of the biggest personalities – always full of questions and excited about the answers.

This particular day I had a new teenage assistant helping me. Duy was a tall, dark, Vietnamese kid with a big smile and a joyful disposition, and because he was a little different, the tots were intrigued.

Spencer, pointing to Duy, asked me about my helper. "What is his name?" Kneeling down, I answered, "Would you like to ask him yourself?" Spencer nodded yes, took my hand, and together we went to find out. "Excuse me," he asked his eyes wide with curiosity. "What is your name?"

"My name? My name is Duy, Duy Tang!" he answered with a big smile. Spencer's face reacted first with a look of surprise, then, a sheepish smile shaded his expression. After a few seconds he said, "Dewy Tang?" ... his nose crinkling, "Now, that's a funny name!"

I laughed, Duy laughed, and Spencer, in all his innocence, laughed along, thrilled that he had somehow entertained us! Out of the mouth of babes, as the old saying goes, comes the obvious truth.

Now, Dick Butkus, that's a funny name!

But there is nothing funny about the image or the iconic status this name represents. Like a four year old, when I first heard this name and saw the NFL image of Dick Butkus, I was intrigued. Actually it was more like in awe.

NFL Films states: "Dick Butkus played football with a religious fervor, with an unrelenting obsession, not to excel, but to dominate and demoralize. For Dick Butkus it was never a game, but a street-fight, a place for all out, no holds barred warfare. Butkus was the most destructive defender in the game and the NFL is filled with stories of men who crossed him. He was a force of unmanageable proportions; he was Moby Dick in a goldfish bowl. His career stands as the most sustained work of devastation ever committed on a football field by anyone, anywhere, at any time."

Dick Butkus is remembered as the toughest man to ever play pro football; a guy who, no matter what, would not quit. He never won a championship or a Super Bowl; hell, his team was so bad they never even made it to a playoff game. That, however, did not stop him from becoming one of the best to ever play NFL Football.

Myself, as a football playing twelve-year old, wanted to be Dick Butkus. Everything from his pigeon toed hulking walk, to the colors of his uniform, was formidable. It all captured my imagination. His linebacker stance, crouching like a mountain lion ready to pounce, was intimidating enough. But when he moved, fully committed, he launched himself with reckless abandon. He was like no other player on the field.

Bob's B.S.

Butkus, for me, became a metaphor for movement and a symbol for effort and accomplishment. No matter what the odds, you never give up. If I invoked my Butkus, I knew what to do, and when to do it.

Now that I've painted a picture of what Butkus looked like and how important he was, I have to tell you, I didn't get it right away. In fact, it took me over thirty years to understand. I had to look deep within my memories to find something I thought I already knew.

And that's the rub! "Having doesn't mean anything if you don't know how to use it" is a topic for a later discussion, but for now, its safe to say, simply knowing something does not make it valuable.

Knowledgeable people are regularly over worked. They tend to be underpaid, and under appreciated, not only by others, but, mostly by themselves.

Michelangelo, the great artist (not the ninja turtle) says "The greater danger for most of us lies not in setting our aim too high and falling short; but setting our aim too low, and achieving the mark!"

Have you been achieving on the low side of what you ask for? Looking for success in all the wrong places? Were you taught, like me, that opportunities take years of suffering to accomplish? They are beyond your control? Were you told to learn more, to create skills you did not have and to go places set by someone else? Then, when you arrived, told again it would be hard, in fact, life was hard. You needed to be tough and learn to put up with what you don't want to get what you do want! Bullshit!

I say what you want, wants you, what you are looking for is looking for you. What you want, doesn't merely exist, more exactly, it already exists inside you. It isn't hard, but yes, it is intense and it does require your full attention! You have heard I am sure, of the natural laws of the universe? I contend the "Law of Attraction" exists not as an external magnet to get you what you want; rather it synchronizes your desires, to bring you more of what you already have.

In the movie "The Lion King," Mufasa calls down from the heavens to his son, Simba, commanding, "Remember who you are!" Your job is to find, perhaps simply to remember, "what" you already possess. What whispers to you will lead you to "Find Your Butkus." Strike that! Remember who you are! Find your own words, find your own ...? in Life! A Buddhist Proverb states, "You already are what you seek."

Like the basic dive play, create an objective you can count on, one that builds confidence. Keep it direct and simple. Remember, it needs to gain a yard whenever you need it, guaranteed! It's your go-to play, the one you use when you are unsure or uncertain. Your dive play maintains your confidence and makes you feel good about yourself.

Self-worth cannot be underestimated. In fact, without it, you will find the simplest tasks to be indomitable challenges. This is why the basic dive play is so important to creating a winning attitude. The formula I use is what I call the W.O.W. factor.

W: Willingness

O: Opportunity

W: Worthiness

My willingness to do creates my opportunity to be worthy. It sounds simple, but the fact is many people are not willing to speak their mind, stand on a principle, or share their most intimate desires. Left unsaid and undone, their dreams never see an opportunity, let alone realize one. Without opportunities, your self worth erodes.

I had my own particular brand of unworthiness. It was more of an OW than a WOW! I looked for Opportunities to be Worthy (O.W.) – always willing to work on other peoples' ideas and projects, while keeping mine in reserve. You could say that I applied myself to external tasks always looking for the payoff, and the worthiness, from someone else.

I suspect that because I had been taught that my creative talent, while interesting, had no true value, I denied myself my greatest power. The mechanics of this are: I could sketch, create and formulate creative, artistic ways of doing just about anything and it was easy for me. In fact, it was too easy. My self-talk told me if something was easy for me, it must not have any value. Practically speaking, my talents were not worthwhile.

My inner dialogue also said, "Everyone knows this stuff, it's common knowledge ... anyone can do this." It's not that it felt unworthy – I just did not give myself any credit. I had been taught that worthwhile things were hard to get and involved hard work. If it was easy, or more correctly stated – "if it was easy for me" it wasn't worth bothering with!

Therefore, instead of expanding on my God given talent to make it world class, I went out of my way to become good at jobs and relationships that were challenging and hard for me. Why take the easy road, when you can choose a more difficult path?

I wonder how many people suffer with this kind of subtle inner defeatism? Are you "WOW-ing" the world or just "OW-ing" yourself? What are you telling yourself?

Worthiness is your day-to-day self-talk. It feeds the opportunities born from your willingness to take action. If you can W.O.W. yourself, you can wow others.

When you work your Dive Play you are creating your W.O.W. Sometimes just gaining a yard when you really need it maintains your self worth and allows you to drive forward to the coming opportunities.

Bob's B.S.
Confidence is attractive and is always in demand.

Just the act of feeling good can put you in the right frame of mind to start noticing what's important. It's not finding out what works in life. No, it's finding your bliss! Joseph Campbell writes, "Follow your bliss and the universe will open doors where only there were walls."

Trust me, if my dream was a guy named Dick Butkus, can what you want be any crazier?

> **Bob's B.S.**
> Open the door to your desires, listen to your field of dreams and then allow all the people, places and things you desire to come to you.
> And they will!

Take-away

> What you are interested in is worthwhile.
> Your self worth is the "dive play" of your life.
> It's your go-to. It is the most basic element of who you are.
> What seems crazy for others is just right for you.
> Use it, be unique – Embrace your oddities!
> W.O.W. - Willingness creates Opportunities that equals Worthiness.
> Your uniqueness is your real power – Uniqueness attracts what you want.
> Confidence is attractive and always in demand!

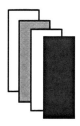

Problems are part of Solutions

Play #3 The Sweep

The Packer Sweep is a play that also builds confidence and, when done well, creates opportunity. The sweep was Vince Lombardi's favorite play - the one he built a dynasty on. Objective: gain 10+ yards. This classic play, originally called the Wing T Buck Sweep, dates back to the earliest beginnings of football.

Hall of Fame running back, Gale Sayers, has a famous quote, "Give me 18 inches. That's all I need." (Meaning: when a play is well executed, even a small opening will allow a great player to "run to daylight.")

The Packer sweep starts with the quarterback pitching the ball to a fast halfback already running towards the outside of the line. Most of the offensive line moves with him, creating strategic blocks and openings to find the gap in the defense. This play is all about creating an opening, then capitalizing on it. There are choices available as the play develops and it is up to the ball carrier to choose the path to success.

An old Indian legend tells this story about choosing a life path:

One evening, an elderly Cherokee brave told his grandson about a battle that goes on inside people. He said, "My son, the battle is between two 'wolves' inside us all. One is evil. It is anger, envy, jealousy, sorrow, regret, greed, arrogance, self-pity, guilt, resentment, inferiority, lies, false pride, superiority, and ego. The other is good. It is joy, peace love, hope serenity, humility, kindness, benevolence, empathy, generosity, truth, compassion and faith." The grandson thought about it for a minute and then asked his grandfather, "Which wolf wins?" The old Cherokee simply replied, "The one that you feed."

Which wolf are you feeding?

I'm not sure that we are equal parts good and evil but we certainly carry all the traits of the wolf. Many times what we feed feels like an involuntary act, seemingly beyond our control. Our unconscious mind is drawn to the strongest emotion. My Sensei taught, "Your mind is 10% conscious intellect and 90% sub-conscious emotion." Take the dilemma of a bad habit, like smoking, drinking or over eating. You know the effects of the habit are harming your health, even killing you. But, because the emotional pleasure/pain centers are activated in the brain, you literally are trying to fight 90% with 10%.

These centers are called the limbic system. A complex set of brain structures located on both sides of the thalamus, near the center of the brain. This system is responsible for endorphin flow, emotion, behavior, motivation and long-term memory. Your emotional life is largely housed in the limbic system, and it has a great deal to do with the formation of memories.

Your memories are essentially the wolf that feeds your desire, be they good or bad. We tend to feed on what is convenient, feasting on what is on-hand and placed in our environment. It's the low hanging fruit of the dominant emotion of the moment, and as a result our thoughts feed upon themselves. While we can't choose the mistakes we make in of our lives, we certainly can choose how we deal with them.

Years ago my environment allowed a dark cloud to rule my life for a time. Unlike Lombardi's Packer Sweep I had put a play in motion without proper preparation and planning. Quickly my plans broke down and I was completely exposed to take a loss. Instead of looking and running for daylight I chose the darkness of defeat. The cloud, however, had a silver lining, as is taught in this lesson.

On a sunny, clear spring morning I was standing on a sidewalk in downtown Parksville. My eyes were lowered, looking down at the pavement. I was under a dark, emotional cloud, and completely oblivious to everything, or anything - except my own depressing thoughts.

Abruptly, a welcoming voice yelled out, "Bobby! Hey, how are you doing?" I turned to see my Karate Sensei coming quickly towards me. Jimmy Mac strode up with his blazing, time-stopping smile and asked, "Bobby, where have you been lately? I haven't seen you in class all week!" Before I could answer, he got right to the point, "Man, you look like shit! Is there something wrong?"

Something wrong? Yes, oh my God, yes, something was wrong! An endless loop of a problem had been winding around in my brain, suffocating me in every way. It was all consuming and demanded my full attention. I was unable to think of anything but my problem.

Seeing my Sensei always reminded me of just how powerful a positive attitude is. MacDonald was a chain-smoking, hard drinking guy about ten years my senior. His energetic, decisive nature made him a real warrior of a man. A Scottish heritage, complete with self-effacing humor, combined with an athletic, wiry 5'10, - 160 lb. build. Jimmy Mac moved like a middleweight and hit like a heavyweight. I loved everything about him and always wished I had his fighting spirit.

Concerned, he stood in front of me, and now he became my first opportunity to say my secret problem out loud. I gushed out what had been tormenting me for the past few weeks. How I hadn't been eating or sleeping. Why my problem was just too much for me, and why there wasn't anything I could do about it!

I was in my early twenties, newly married, and building a new home for my bride. I had found a special building plan and worked out my idea of a budget. I had grandiose ideas of the magnificent creation I was undertaking, but frankly I hadn't spent much time on the cost details of my new project.

About three quarters of the way finished, I realized I had gone over budget and run out of mortgage money. Worse than that, I still owed ten thousand dollars of outstanding bills, now due, to sub contractors. I was embarrassed and humiliated. I had caused this, and it was all due to my own stupidity. I thought I would lose the house, my equity, my reputation, but worst of all, my friends. Everything I had been working so hard for would now be lost! I had gone to the bank to see if they would lend me more money but they said, "Sorry, we can only give you the funds that we had already agreed upon."

It was hopeless. I was hopeless.

Each night I lay in bed with my stomach turning and my brain spinning. The same questions circled in my brain, "What am I going to do about this problem? I don't have any more money. I can't get any. What is going to happen? How did I let this happen?! Why was I so stupid?"

Not great questions for your confidence and self-esteem. As I finished telling my problems to Sensei, I felt like a beaten dog. I cowered, waiting for Jim to tell me that my problem was unsolvable. Furthermore, I expected him to confirm that I was probably the stupidest, worst person to ever walk in shoe leather.

Jimmy Mac watched and listened patiently as he inhaled the last drag of his spent cigarette. On the exhale he said, "Bobby, I was really worried about you. I thought you had cancer or something. Man, you really had me scared! Ten grand, geesh, what's that house worth? I know you do good work and it sounds like there's lots of equity there. I think those assholes at the bank are screwing with you - because you're young."

On his next breath he continued, "You know what I would do? I'd go there and tell those turkeys at the bank that you want the ten grand to finish the house! You have the equity and if they don't agree to do it right now, you are walking away from the project, unfinished, and you're going on welfare! Screw them and their bag of snakes!"

Then, just as quickly as he appeared with his positive, never-say-die energy, he was on to his next stop. When my head stopped spinning, my feet started moving! Unconsciously, I began walking towards the bank. "Yes, screw them and their bag of snakes," I thought, and my mind opened to all the possibilities.

In the next moment, the weight fell off my shoulders, the clouds parted, and the sun was warm again. I was in the bank manager's office within the hour and had a commitment for obtaining the needed funds within 24 hours.

I spent countless days consumed by what I thought was an unsolvable problem. Tony Robbins calls it the "endless loop" problem syndrome. If you keep asking the wrong questions over and over, you will stop looking for the right answers. All you do is create more and bigger problems. Like attracts like. I was depressed for weeks over a problem that was solved within minutes, by simply looking at it differently. The strong immobilizing emotions of fear and lack were immediately replaced by the action and doing.

My Karate Sensei had taught me one of the most important lessons of my life.

Bob's B.S.
Problems are part of the solutions. They are, in fact, the crucial first half of success, and action is the key to solving them.

Movement is life. Stagnation is death. Never lock on the problem. Always move, take action, and focus on the solution.

The next day, I set a new rule for myself. I decided never again to worry about money! If I ever had another financial problem, I would give myself thirty minutes of 100% worry time. Then, I would make a decision of what to do and take the necessary action to get it done. To this day I have followed my rule to the letter, giving myself thirty minutes to come to a decision. Then taking whatever action seems to be the best.

If, on the following day, my action turns out to be the wrong decision, I simply give myself 30 more minutes and come up with a new solution! No self-doubt, no self-inflicted beatings, and no endless worry. Just take action, move forward, and find a positive outcome.

The wolf you feed does not discriminate between good and bad, right and wrong, the wolf simply eats. It's just hungry. You have the choice to feed the problem or the solution.

Got a problem? Give yourself about thirty minutes to limit your down side, and always think about what you want to have happen.

Look for an opening. Find a way to succeed, even if it is just for a moment. Run to daylight! Never let the problem rule your thoughts. Use the emotion of action. Use the 90% to overwhelm the worries of inaction.

Take-away

Every situation has light & darkness.
Look for the opening; find the opportunity. Run to daylight.
Action and movement defeat worry.
Worry is intellectual, 10%. Action is emotional, 90%
Accept your problem. Honor it with thought.
Take 30 minutes of worry. Decide on a solution, any solution, and then take action immediately.

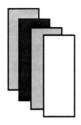

The Three Questions

Play #4 The Texas Option

Good things come in threes. The Veer or the "Texas Option" is a quick-hitting run that has multiple options. Objective: 10+ yards. The football is handled by the quarterback, who runs, veers away from the defense. He can hand it off or fake it to the fullback who dives into the line, or he keeps the ball – deciding whether to run or pitch the ball to a ready half back who is running behind him. This can create a great deal of confusion for both the defense and the offense. Here, trained instincts are the key to knowing what to do.

You gotta have poise in the noise!

As there are three different options, at three different times within in one play, the key is to answer the question of what to do and then do it without thinking. Develop the instinct of just doing.

The power of three is also a lesson that was first introduced to me when Sensei asked:

"What is the sound of one hand clapping?"

"What was your face before your mother was born?"

"Does a dog have a Buddha nature?"

Richard Kim, a 9th degree Black Belt, was world-renowned for his teachings and for his books about Zen and the Martial Arts. At the time I first met him, Kim was a karate man in his seventies who, along with his multiple PHD degrees in history and psychology, was a Shinto priest and Tai Chi Master. He was the man who coined the ideal of being an "artist of life" and demonstrated the essence of being a leader. For me, although I enjoyed the karate training, it was his lectures and his talks that ranged from classic samurai stories, to modern medicine and religion that fascinated me.

One of his favorite lessons was to evoke the three Zen Koans and then weave them thoughtfully into his lectures. He called them the riddles that lead to Satori, the Japanese word for enlightenment.

"What is the sound of one hand clapping?" Kim asked, his eyes shining with mischief. Then he smiled, looked at his audience and answered his own question. "My student, Peter Urban, says – da' left hook! It's the left hook – that's the sound of one hand clapping. Da left hook works every time!"

Always enjoying his own joke, Sensei would put his hands on his knees and roar with laughter. This, of course, would elicit his audience to do the same and then at the peak of joy, shifting gears, he would become serious, and then share his wisdom with the audience. "You cannot try to solve the riddle though," his expression now deeper. "There is not an intellectual answer, only a spiritual one. To answer the riddle of the Koan, you need only ask the question and then let your unconscious mind unravel the riddle."

Looking for the answers to questions without thinking? Without judgment? How?

Perhaps it is just being, rather than doing. Perhaps it's living in the moment with complete focus, but devoid of any direction. Zen: the emptiness of everything. The Buddhist saying, "The longest journey you can take is from your head to your heart", or "less is more" comes to mind. These ideas sound to me like the concentrated efforts of a monk or the gifted thoughts of a scholar, not thoughts for the everyday man.

Bob's B.S.

Yet, this is where the extraordinary lies: in the ordinary! You do not have to climb up a mountain to find yourself.

You are right here, right now and everything you are or can be already exists within you. No one else in the entire world knows what you know. No one! To engage the power of the universe, all you need is to notice the value of your own experiences.

Psychologists state there are three levels of consciousness. The totality of our consciousness is comprised of these three levels: the subconscious, the conscious, and the super-conscious. These levels of consciousness represent the differing degrees of awareness.

The first level, the subconscious, is relatively dim in awareness. This is the stuff of which dreams are made. We may think of it as our remembered experiences or impressions of what has happened to us. Our feelings are just that: remembered experiences that we hold in our body. Finding them in our gut or within our heart.

The next level of consciousness from which we receive guidance is the conscious state, the rational awareness that guides our daily decisions. When we receive input from the senses, analyze the facts, and make decisions based on this information, we are using this conscious level of guidance.

This process is also strongly affected by the opinions of others, which can cloud our ability to think for ourselves. Here is where we need our defensive plays to guide and protect us from unwanted information and opinions.

Finally, intuition and heightened mental clarity flow from the third level, the super-conscious. The conscious mind is limited by its analytical nature, and therefore sees all things as separate and distinct. When we try to consciously analyze a certain situation, we may become puzzled because our problem seems singular in its nature. Much like the old saying "You can't see the forest for the trees!"

By contrast, because the super-conscious mind is all inclusive and sees all things as part of a whole, it can readily draw solutions. In super-consciousness, the problem and the solution are seen as one, as though the solution is a natural outgrowth from the problem. Have you ever noticed that your eyes tend to roll up, and look up when you are seeking an answer? Who are you talking to?

The ancient Hawaiians have a word called "Huna". Like the Japanese "Ki" or the "Chinese "Chi", Huna means life force. The life force is described by creating three separate circles. The conscious mind is centered between the feeling unconscious and the intuitive super-conscious mind. The conscious mind reaches down, or within to feel and accesses the super-conscious through the unconscious. Basically meaning you cannot access your intuition, your super-conscious, God-like mind without trusting your feelings and asking for direction.

You have to ask!

Three Levels of Awareness

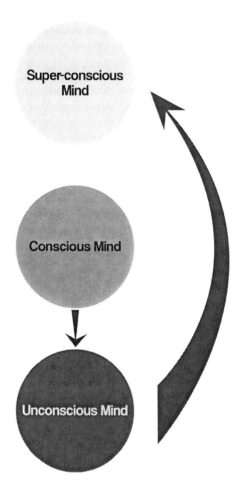

During my 'self-studies' to understand the riddles of my own life, I have occasionally found a few answers. In turn these few answers have always led to more questions! A news writer might say, "Answer the W5 questions when you tell a story. Who? What? Where? When? Why? How?"

I was also taught by various business organizations to know

what your "Why" is. If your why is big enough, it will in turn, fuel your desires to achieve what you want. This makes sense on the surface, but frankly when I hear someone ask why? I hear Whining! Why is this? Why is that? Why did this happen to me? Poor me. Why, why, why?! It just opens up more defeatist questions than I feel it solves. For me, why doesn't matter so much. Why? Because, it is what it is. Deal with it and move on.

Remove the negative whining and re-frame your "why" thoughts into actions filled with what and how reasons rather than why excuses. I don't care why something happened. I only care what I can do about it. My own three questions occurred to me much like Sensei's riddles, as they have come from a spectrum of teachers and from my many and varied experiences.

Bob's B.S.
Discover what vibrates for you and you'll find your Butkus.
The three questions are:
What is a perfect Sound?
What would you do, if you knew you could not fail?
What do you want?

Once you know what you want, then the how and where to find your heart's desire seems to fall into place. I would not ask, "Why was I born?"

My question is "What was I born to do!?" Do the work, ask yourself; "What do I want, and what am I interested in doing to get what I want?" Then listen for the sound or, more accurately, the vibration of 'what' feels like perfection to you. Each person has a unique vibration, a perfect note, one that resonates with your true self. Notice what it is, take it in and savor it when something good happens, then appreciate how you feel.

Here is a simple exercise: At the top of piece of paper write: "What is my true purpose in life?" Then, as quickly as you can, write an answer, any answer that comes to you. It doesn't have to be a complete sentence. Repeat this over and over until you write the answer that makes you feel emotional. This is your purpose, when you feel it; you will have your perfect note.

That's it. It doesn't matter if you're a counsellor, or an engineer, or a bodybuilder. To some people this exercise will make perfect sense. To others it will seem utterly stupid. Usually it takes 15-20 minutes to clear your head of all the clutter, to discover what you think your purpose in life is. The false answers will come from your mind and your memories. But when the true answer finally arrives, it will feel like it's coming to you from beyond. You may actually vibrate with excitement or possibly cry with release.

"Continuous effort - not strength or intelligence - is the key to unlocking our potential." Winston Churchill

As Sensei Kim taught in his riddles, "No one can help you discover the sound of one hand clapping and you can't consciously think of what the answer might be."

What you want must stir your soul; wake you up from a dead sleep, and ring so harmoniously loud in your ears that you cannot hear anything or anyone else. This is your vibration, your note, your perfect note and it is everything.

What-do-you-want?

Take-away

> Be an artist of life.
> Tap into your intuition, super-conscious mind.
> The extraordinary lies in the ordinary.
> Ask yourself consciously what you want, feel your desire deeply in the unconscious. Listen for the answer, without judgment, from the super-conscious mind.
> Discovering your "what" is your purpose.
> Take 20 minutes and ask for an answer

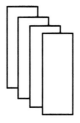

Do You Want It, Yes or No?

Play #5 The Draw

Heads or tails? At the flip of a coin you have to decide which side you are on. The draw play starts like a slow motion coin flipping in the air. A disguised run, initially it looks like a pass play. Objective: 10+ yards. The offensive linemen draw back like they're going to pass-protect for the quarterback. The quarterback also drops back, but instead of setting up to pass, he turns and hands the ball to the runner. A simple deflection-play, where it is unclear who will get the football. In the draw play you have to decide whether to pass or to run.

Knowing you have an option, the key remains to be decisive. Many times in the heat of battle or in a moment of need, you simply have no time to think. Both options can work. Opportunities, like the draw-option, often come disguised as something unexpected or in an unusual way. Acting with instinct requires training and self-belief. There comes a moment in the play where you must trust your gut and put all your faith into an action.

To do or not to do.

The elements are the same for all. "The same boiling water that softens the potato hardens the egg." It's about what you are made of, not the circumstances.

One of my first option plays, should I pass or should I run, began after lunch on a fresh April day in 1975. The boss and I went to Stewart & Hudson Building Supply to pick up some materials for the afternoon's work. On the way back, he took a detour down a street I'd never been and stopped in front of two vacant building lots. The boss, Russ Horsnell, was a big man, 6'1, around 200 lbs. He was about 40 years old with an unusually quiet demeanor for a construction guy. In fact, he was down right quiet, rarely making small talk, preferring instead, to let his actions speak for themselves. So when he began to tell me about his future plans, it came as a surprise.

Just fourteen months earlier he had hired me, a green 16-year-old kid, with a grade eleven education, to be his newest apprentice. Hell, I don't know why he ever took a chance on me or, for that matter, how I wound up as a carpenter's helper. I had no aptitude for woodworking. I was afraid of heights, and I knew nothing about construction. Even the power tools scared me! Never the less, Russ was a quiet guy who seemed to like strays, so I guess I was a fit.

He looked at me and then over towards two freshly cleared lots saying, "We're going to build a couple of small ranchers on those lots. Each will be about 960 sq. ft., with 3 bedrooms and will have cedar siding. We'll build them at the same time, so we can keep the costs down." "This one," he said, pointing to the closest lot, "We'll put on the market for $34,900.00. We'll keep the price low, so we can sell it before it's finished." Then he paused for a moment, and offered, "The second one will be a good starter house for a young person, so I think you should buy it. Since we are saving a little money by doing them at the same time, you can have it for $30,000."

Then, there was absolute silence. The only sound I heard was of my heart thumping as I sat there with a vacant look on my face. Then came the question, which I have always remembered, "Do you want it? Yes or no?"

Before I give you the answer let's jump ahead to the lessons I learned from karate that would help me later on. Mentors, leaders, and teachers show up in many different and unexpected ways. However, an expected teacher was a man named Richard Kim, 9th Dan/Hanshi. Every year, O'Sensei Kim lectured about life and taught traditional Karatedo at an annual summer camp held at the University of Guelph. One evening, after a particularly tough day of training, Kim began his nightly lecture, talking about the basics. He taught that, in life, the basics are the foundation of all accomplishments and of all advanced skills and thoughts.

"Take the opening line-up and bows," he began. "At the start of every class, we begin with a traditional Samurai bow." On the command to line-up, everyone would run to his or her spot in the dojo. The Sensei would be at the front, facing the students, with the advanced Black Belts forming a line to his left. The Kyu belts, or colored belts, would create lines directly facing the Sensei. The most senior student or belt level would stand in the Sempai or first student position. After that, each student would line up according to his/her present rank in the class. Brown belts are followed by blue belts, who are followed by a green belts and so on down the line.

The Japanese, like the Germans, love precision and order. As in all cultural distinctions, learning Martial Arts has many lessons about military virtue and honor, thus the line-up was very much like soldiers learning to march on a parade ground. The line-up also included a philosophy, and a specific meaning for each and every action.

"Your superior is to your right and your subordinate is to your left. Everyone needs a good right hand man, just as someone must always be, left in charge," chuckled Kim. "In life, you think of yourself as being in the middle. You respect the person ahead of you and you have compassion for the person behind you. When you understand these two equal thoughts, you can begin to develop a sense of gratitude."

"Respect, compassion and gratitude are the three tenets of the opening bows. Your class begins and ends with a bow, a courtesy, and that is how you give thanks for your life," continued Kim. Then we would descend like a big domino line, kneeling down in perfect order to the "seiza" position. After everyone was seated, we would begin the three traditional samurai bows.

"Shoman ni rei," a bow to the past generations of teachers, was the first bow. With great ceremony, each student would then bow in order. Each person placed their left hand first on the tatami floor, then their right, followed by a full-face bow onto the hands. Then, returning to the seated position, the right hand lifted first, then the left, your spine was straight and the chin slightly tucked with as much decorum and dignity as possible. Next, the most senior student would loudly yell, "Mokso!" Everyone, including the Sensei, would close his/her eyes in a brief silent prayer and meditation.

"Focus on your breath, "O'Sensei would teach. "During mokuso, you meditate, giving thanks for your life in a very specific order. First, you are thankful for your good friend, then your country, and finally your God."

I always thought this was an odd order, as most religions

would put God first. But here he asked us to be grateful for the things closest to our lives. That is why you give thanks for your good friend first. Your good friend could be a parent, a mentor, a co-worker, or someone you had just met. The important part of the good friend is to notice and be grateful for that special relationship and impact that they have in your life. Your country is not simply a flag - it is the entire world and universe. Give thanks to nature and all its abundance because it nurtures you with your every action. Finally, look inside to your heart and know that you have a "Buddha nature." You are god and as god is an internal perception of your heart, not an external manifestation of your mind, it is a completely personal experience. That is why it is placed third.

"Finally," Kim stated, "you must understand that the line-up is a representation of your life. You get exactly as you deserve. When you come into the dojo for the first time, you start as an equal. Everyone works, nothing is free, and everyone starts at the beginning, at the back of the line. Then, only through your own efforts, do you advance. You must do the work to get ahead. Your training is not just to be a martial artist, but rather to be an "artist of life!" The bows were the foundation of the training. Anything built without a proper foundation cannot stand up to what it may be asked to endure.

What I might endure or rather what I might become began with a question. The poet, Robert Browning asked, "Ah, but a man's reach should exceed his grasp, or what's a heaven for?"

It wasn't heaven asking me to stretch, rather it was Russ's question that was hard to grasp. Like the option play in football I had to decide whether to pass or run? And I had to do it right now!

"So, do you want it? Yes or no?" Russ asked

To use the baseball vernacular, I didn't know whether to "shit or steal third." It was very surprising to me when, with very little hesitation, I simply said, "Yes." Internally, I had a thousand questions. How could I ...? What do I ...? When do I ...? Who will ...? All that came out was, "Yes." There was no qualifying and certainly no questioning, just a simple choice, yes or no? What do you want?

"Yes, I will do that," I agreed.

"Good," he said. "I'll figure out all the details." For the next three months we built the two houses. I felt the sense of pride of ownership and began to take a keener interest in how all the pieces were put together. Perhaps that was part of the lesson, as well as the helping hand, that Russ wanted me to learn.

When the house was built, Russ arranged an agreement of sale for me. Being only seventeen years old, I was too young to obtain a mortgage. Then, he borrowed the money and lent it to me. He was the guarantor and I made monthly payments directly to the bank. Due to the extraordinary gesture and helping hand from a man I had only known a short time, I moved into my first house before my eighteenth birthday.

For 10 years I would learn the building business with help from Russ. He assisted me to start my own company and he became a life-long friend and mentor. I watched how he built things and more importantly, how he organized his work, treated his customers, and managed the sub trades with whom he dealt. His teaching and lessons created a strong foundation for each of my future professions and ambitions.

I had the opportunity, later in life, to ask this man why? I had asked him about the dozens of young men he had hired as apprentices during his career. More specifically, why did he hire me and once he saw that I was so poor at the job – why did he keep me?

Russ admitted with a smile "Yes, you were about the worst kid I ever saw – basically useless as an apprentice – at first. You couldn't do anything."

I'll admit I was a little taken aback and surprised at his candor. Then he continued "But, you did have one thing, and there you were the best. You were willing! No matter what I asked you to do, you would try, never complain, and you would not quit. I'll take willingness over talent every day, all day, every time!"

That was a good "why" and a better story, one I have taught many, many times. Sitting in Russ's truck that afternoon, I had been thankful for a good friend by respecting his trust and compassion for me. Saying "yes" to an opportunity was a habit I started on that day.

Years later, as I formed my skills as an effective teacher, I found the gratitude of the moment that Russ had created. I had always thanked him for the opportunity that he provided, but as a martial arts teacher, I saw the lesson of the moment from a different angle.

Bob's B.S.
The easy answer in that moment would have been to say, "No," and to deny both Russ' and my own abilities.

Not trusting what was being offered, or allowing the "what ifs" to dictate, would have created very different results.

Although it would be a decade or so before I would hear O'Sensei's lecture, this moment represented my first bow.

I said, "Yes," and not for any practical reason. It happened so fast that I had no time to prepare. Like the draw-option play I had to decide to accept the ball or let it be passed to someone else. My answer was based completely on trust and faith. When my superior made a compassionate gesture, I responded with respect, and we are both grateful for the friendship that followed.

My first bow was a good one.

Take-away

Opportunities abound in unplanned and unexpected ways.
Respect + Compassion = Gratitude.
Trust & learn to say yes more than no.
Willingness is more important than talent-ness.

Three Thousand Miles To Say No

Play #6 The Bomb

How far you will go depends on how far you can throw! Our final play is the "Bomb!" It's the most exciting play in the game. Objective: 50 yards/touchdown. The quarterback drops back to pass, seeing his receivers streak down the field as far and as fast as they can go. The quarterback throws the football as far as he can, trusting the chosen receiver will make the catch. This is a low percentage play that requires perfect timing and an all out attitude for success. But it is not a Hail Mary, or a wish of a play – no, it is the will to win with pure talent and desire.

Everything is on the line.

Trickery is not involved, as everyone in the stadium can see it happening. It's pure art, win or lose, either a touchdown or an interception!

"He who works with his hands is a laborer. He who works with his hands and his head is a craftsman. He who works with his hands and his head and his heart is an artist." - St. Francis of Assisi

When you put everything on the line, all of your being into your task, you don't have time to think about failure. The excitement, the danger, and the outright exhilaration of being "all in" create immediate gratification, and success typically follows. Deciding what you want, then doing it requires your heart, your head, and your hands. You gotta do the work and take your chances.

Sometimes you just gotta "Throw the Bomb!"

As I reared back to throw one of the longest passes of my life, I was asked a challenging question, "Bob, I know that you want to do your 'kung fu' stuff, but I understand that you are a pretty good builder, so would you like to have the job?"

The timing could not have been better. It was the spring of 1984 and as the Ontario winter snow melted, this was a tremendous offer, a gift actually.

Three years before had been a very different time, as economic and biological circumstances had created a sense of lack and fear in me, and in my new bride, Paula Staite. Her baby announcement earlier that year had elicited a less than happy response from me. I thought the timing was bad, and said so. 1981 was a bad year that was about to get worse, as interest rates peaked to a record 21%. The local and national economy was devastated.

I was on my own now, working my little contracting business called 'PB Construction.' That's 'Parksville Bob Construction.' I always liked to have a little fun with everything I did, so for me, although the name was fun, right now the business was not. I was 24 years old. I was young and naive. I didn't really understand why the interest rates were destroying the business community. All I knew was that by June of 1981, there was no work and very little money. I watched as almost every one of the truly established builders in Parksville, B.C. went broke.

My old boss, Russ, survived the recession because he was

smart and careful. I did because I had little to lose. We both survived the year by a very slim margin. That said, as I looked for carpentry jobs during the day, I scrambled to make a little extra cash with the part time Karate club in the evening. There were no carpentry jobs to be had, so a little bit of karate club cash and a line of credit from the bank sustained our living. Paula and I often joked that if it were not for the loose change she found in the cushion cracks of the couch, we would not have eaten.

Like all things in life, you find a way to survive and you get through it. By the end of the year I had my first son, Leigh. Although initially he had a funny head from the trauma of a two-day birth, he was, in my opinion, the most beautiful baby ever born. By the following spring, the business was starting to recover and I created a plan to recoup my losses.

For the next two years I would build one speculation house, the same plan, over and over. I was lucky and I was careful. I threw myself into the plan of building each house as if I would move in. However, if I could sell it before completion, I would do so and build again from the same plan. It worked and I worked, building during the day and teaching karate part time in the evenings.

I was happy with the renewed success of my building business, but I had lost faith and lost interest in making this my life's work. To me, having watched the established builders get wiped out the year before was a lesson that I wanted to learn from. This was a very unfair business – always feast or famine. I didn't want to wind up as a forty year old who had been wiped out because of some idiotic mistakes by the government or from the general greed of the world.

So, like most young people, I came to a crossroads early in my life. As Yogi Berra, the NY Yankee's great, liked to say,

"When you see a fork in the road - take it!"

It was time to make a change, but what kind of change? I found myself asking, "What do I know how to do? What are my options?" Perhaps I need to get some more education and I should go back to school?" When I had that thought, I immediately sat down and waited until the thought went away! Having quit school after grade 11, I wasn't exactly the scholarly type. For me, school, outside of art and sports, had always been a struggle. I was basically a C- student. My own opinion of myself was that I could barely read and write. Math? Forget about it. Anything past simple addition and subtraction seemed to be a huge challenge for me.

The only thing I knew, besides pounding nails was a little bit of punching and kicking. At 25 years old, I knew I needed to learn more. The karate club was at least a start, but I had never seen any real success there.

Years before, I had watched my teacher, Sensei Jimmy Mac, who was far better than I; struggle to make even the simplest of livelihoods. I had taken over his part time club when he wanted to move to Florida and sail a boat. I took it on only because no one else wanted it and, as the top student in the dojo, I felt obligated.

With the club only bringing in about $500 dollars a month in cash, this was not much of a business. Besides, if a great teacher like MacDonald couldn't succeed, what chance did I have?

When the universe closes a door, she opens a window. Now, because of my need for change, I was presented with a host of teachers and opportunities. Suddenly I found a partner, Rick Marshall. Together we took the part time club to being a full time school.

He introduced me to Sensei Don Warrener, Hanshi

Richard Kim, and Master Don Jacob. These were successful businessmen teaching martial arts, and I became one of them. When I was around them I felt like I knew less than nothing, but I absorbed everything. I became a knowledge- seeking sponge. Warrener, in particular, treated me well, as I think he felt sorry for me. Honestly, I believe that he saw nothing in me. To him, I could barely even punch and kick! I knew nothing and knew nobody. It would be no skin off his nose to throw me a bone or two.

I joined Richard Kim's 'Zen Bei Butoku Kai' organization. Although I had already earned my 2nd Degree, Nidan Black Belt with Bateson Karate. I was told that I needed to retest for my Shodan – 1st Degree Black Belt. Many would have taken this as an insult. I saw it simply as what I needed to do. Kim not only required a physical test, but he made you write a 1,000 word essay for him with your philosophic thoughts on "What does Karatedo mean to me?" I had not written as much as a word for almost ten years. I can still feel the intimidation I felt as I thought, "1,000 words? Oh my god! My philosophy? What philosophy? He wants it double spaced and typed too!"

Interestingly, because I now co-owned the local Karate School, I was considered a leader. Regardless of what they really thought of me, I was afforded equal treatment as a peer, not a student. Although this created all kinds of problems for me as I struggled to understand things that I had never been taught; it made me stretch myself and go beyond my doubts. I simply had no choice, either buck up or wither and fail.

I was beyond humble in the presence of these successful men and I was ready to completely start over. If I could learn from their success, I could change my life, and that is what I did. As my construction business began to make me a living again; I worked on creating my exit strategy.

In the summer of 1983, as I was about to build my parents their new dream home in Nanaimo B.C., I announced to them, "This will be the last house that I ever build. When I finish this, Paula (now pregnant again) and I are selling everything and moving 3,000 miles across Canada to her home town of Brockville Ontario, and starting a full time Karate School and Fitness business."

"Why would you do that?" Dad asked, as his hand went to his forehead in disbelief. "You have a successful business here and you are good at it. You have really done it now! This is crazy!"

Paraphrasing Forrest Gump, "Momma says, crazy is as crazy does!" By the spring of 1984 I had a new daughter, Brittany, and I had sold everything we owned.

Now I was standing in the living room of my brother in-law, Rick Paquin's Brockville home. Rick offered, "Bob, I know that you want to do your 'kung fu' stuff, but I understand that you are a pretty good builder, so would you like to have the job?"

Rick Paquin, overweight, overbearing, and seemingly always glassy eyed, was a country smart, "good old boy" businessman and very successful. I liked him immediately, as he had a bigger than life laugh and as smart as a fox. Paquin had made his money in a series of gas stations, along with buying and selling real estate. He was tough and he measured everyone he met.

He worked hard, drank even harder and he loved to, in the friendliest way, show off. Rick loved Elvis, makin' deals, makin' money and he loved Dru, Paula's sister. However, he couldn't stand the rest of the Staite family as, from his experience, he saw them as freeloaders. When he met me, he didn't know where I stood or what I was made of. During my time in Brockville he would become an invaluable ally to whom I give credit as being the original author of many of my business ideas. Yes, he was that smart and that good!

It was my first night in Brockville and here I was confronted with an offer that I could not or should not refuse. "When are you going to start your Karate School?" Rick asked.

"Not until the fall," I found myself saying. "The summer time is not a good time to start this kind of business, so I'll start looking for a suitable retail space and be ready to rock and roll by September."

"That sounds like a plan." Liking what he heard, Rick offered, "Last fall I put in the foundation for my new water-front home and as soon as the frost clears I'll begin construction. Hell, I know everyone in town so I'll be my own contractor on this, but you know what, I like you already and I understand that you are one hell of a good framer. Sounds like you have the time, so if you want the job, it's yours!"

Before I could answer, he continued "I've got some quotes right now for about five grand to frame it up to lock up. I can get you a couple of swampers to help you, so if you're in, let's shake on it and then we'll have another drink."

It was early April and he was right. I did have the time and five thousand dollars was a lot of money to me, especially in 1984. It would basically feed the family until the fall while paying for the move east. This was a tremendous opportunity!

As I pondered Rick's offer I considered putting off my decision and talking to my wife, with the idea of sleeping on it to answer him in the morning.

A martial arts lesson came to mind. Many people think that it was Julius Caesar who, after crossing the Rubicon, burned his boats as a motivational tool for his soldiers. In 1519, the actual event happened, when a Spaniard General named Hernan Cortes conquered the Aztec nation. The legend states that he burned his only method of retreat, his ships, on the beaches that one day would be Mexico. He and his men would have to win and defeat the indigenous people, or they would die.

I have never been in the habit of burning my bridges, but this was different. I was about to suggest that I would consider this and get back to him in the morning, when alternate words started to flow.

"Rick, I don't have to sleep on this or think about it," I stammered a little, "…and I can't tell you just how much I appreciate this offer. It's really something and I thank you!"

His eyes narrowed, and his jaw tightened just a little, "But?" he said, with a slight raise in his voice.

"But, no. I hung up my nail pouch last month and I sold everything I had to travel 3,000 miles to be the Sensei and to follow my dreams. I don't know if I will succeed, but if all I accomplish is surviving the next five years by being the Sensei, then that is what I will do and it's good enough for me."

Rick unfurrowed his forehead, his narrowed eyes relaxed, and he roared with laughter. "You wild SOB! You are crazy! You know there have been two karate guys here before you, and they both failed! I love it! You got nothin' and you stand here and you tell me that you don't need me! Well, son, you are OK with me! Let's get that drink!"

With that, I knew that I had left the bridges intact, but there was no turning back. I really didn't understand just how much I believed in myself until that moment. I had staked my claim, planted the flag, and told the universe that I had arrived and that I was a warrior.

From that point forward I immersed my being in the study of "self" to understand the psychology of success. As a student Sensei, I would develop my own uniqueness and philosophies about karate and, more importantly, about life.

Years later I would hear business teacher, Brian Tracy say, "If it's going to be, it's up to me."

Take-away

Look inside yourself for the resources you need to succeed
Be fully committed –be all in.
Don't be distracted by anything that may change your own self worth.
People and opportunities will support and believe in you: when they see you, believe in you.
Throw the Bomb – Expect to Score!

1972 Saanich Hornets team photo. 1986 with Leigh –
Karate Photo. 15 yrs. old - ready for a league game.

1987 with Sensei Richard Kim. 1997 Family Karate with Leigh, Brit, Drew & Kieran. 1976 as an orange belt - demonstration with Sensei Jimmy Mac.

Finding his Butkus earns
Kelowna man Emmy award

**Local artist featured in
award-winning NFL Films documentary**

By DON PLANT
The Daily Courier

Kelowna painter Bob Mueller returned home from New York Wednesday clutching an Emmy award.

The artist's inspirational story impressed the judges so much, the 11-minute film, Finding Your Butkus, beat out five other documentaries to win this year's award for outstanding long sports feature on television.

25 years, he has spoken to groups of karate students for four years. His main message: follow your dreams, no matter how silly they seem.

"If I can make something out of this, then how silly are your dreams? They can't be as silly as this one," he said in March.

No one from NFL Films was optimistic the documentary would win. The other nominees dealt with more tragic material, including the death of former San Francisco 49ers coach Bill Walsh and a Kentucky Derby horse that broke a leg and had to be put down.

"Then they got this sunshiny piece about a guy who

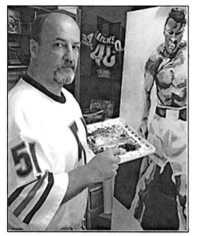

Kelowna painter Bob Mueller and his son-in-law, Leith Pedersen, had seats on the New England Patriots' goal line in the fourth quarter of the Super Bowl, so they had a close-up view of the game-winning touchdown.

Kelowna sports artist gets 'super' exposure at Super Bowl events

Previous page: 2010 with Dick Butkus at the Butkus Awards. With Steve Sabol at NFL Films. This page: Painting Ali. Characture art by Glen Hughes. At Super Bowl 42 with Leith. News articles via Kelowna Daily Courier.

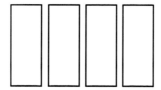

The Four Quarters

There are stages to everything. If we consider the whole of something, we can usually find a way to divide it into more manageable pieces. Like the old joke asking "How do you eat an elephant?" The answer is, "One bite at a time!" Our life is like the elephant. If we chew on it piece by piece, we'll de able to digest each bite, enjoying both the taste and the sustenance.

The choices here can be split it half, separated into thirds or cut it into quarters. Of course we can take it further and completely slice and dice the whole, but for my purposes: ""Finding Your Butkus"" is carved into quarters. Like the game I love, every section proves to have purpose. Each quarter provides its own meaning, while it establishes a foundation for the future. During a pre-game pep talk, the 'Hall of Fame' Coach of the Dallas Cowboys liked to say,

"Feel 'em out in the first quarter, establish yourself in the second, take command in the third, and put 'em away in the fourth."- Tom Landry via Steve Sabol.

Like a football game, there are many examples of various quarters that give us direction. Our seasons: spring, summer, fall and winter are the most noticeable quarters we follow in life. In turn, our life has stages like childhood, teenage, adult and senior. The Indian Hindu philosophy speaks of the four ashrama or ages: the student, the householder, then hermitage and the ascetic age. The first three stages are life affirming and common to all: a childhood to learn from, adulthood for responsibility, and then a senior, retirement for rest. The forth is reserved for the enlightened few who break with tradition, and reject the first three stages of life. They reject comfort and embrace austerity while letting go of any form of possession. Not many of us will be a Ghandi or a Mother Theresa, but if we see our life as a whole we will enter into a reflective forth stage. The final stage usually brings with it a sense of wisdom. This reflective experience shows us how the quarters played out and why they were so important to the outcome.

While we may not become "enlightened" from the actions of the active stages of our life, the idea of redemption and understanding is one that we can all share. This is where I see the value. Not in rejecting our past, but by embracing our journey to discover its lessons and perhaps its hidden joys.

Bob's B.S.
The game of life is just that, a game, and a game is meant to be played.

In the first chapters I set out a few simple stories with a basic set of principles and beliefs. These stories are the foundational experiences I had during the student age. The early householder age had even more lessons, but "Finding Your Butkus" did not become a reality until later in life. Thus my four quarters begin here and now!

Yes, life is a game, so let's play!

The four quarters are, as they are in a football game, divided equally with each holding an important role in the outcome.

Bill Shankley states, "Some people think football is a matter of life and death. I assure you, it's much more important than that!"

The first quarter is how you start, thus it's "the Kickoff."
The second quarter, "the Game Plan," is all about strategy and learning about the competition. The third quarter, the "Ball Control," is often tumultuous with an ebb and flow that is based on momentum and circumstance. The fourth quarter, the outcome, is all about late game heroics – thus it's "the 4th Quarter Comeback!"

After each quarter you need to review the "play by play" analysis and determine the takeaways. Look to see which plays were used, their effectiveness, and how they affected the game plan. I leave this to your imagination to see how many plays you can find in the stories. The only way you can improve your game is to look at all the individual plays, successful or not, and learn from them!

The following chapters are The Four Quarters that lead to the discovery of "Finding Your Butkus." They are the football/ life game I played over a period of, interestingly enough, four years. The discovery, development, revival and redemption all seemed like random events while they happened, but when seen as quarters of a contest the pattern is undeniable.

The four stages of the hero appear, as Joseph Campbell predicts they will.

Nothing is random in the universe. Everything matters and there are no accidents!

Take-away

Choose a story from your life and divide
the experience into four quarters.
Look at the events and create a heroic journey for yourself.

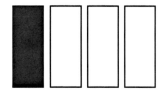

Having Doesn't Mean Anything

- if you don't know how to use it!

The First Quarter

The Kick Off is the most anticipated part of the game, full of match ups and mystery. The players and the coaches know every detail of the game plan and have been preparing for their opponents all week. The fans are restless, and the excitement is palpable.

In 1967 Steve Sabol wrote, "Pro-football - it begins with a whistle and ends with a gun!" Drama exists before each new start. Anticipation is hope, and hopeful fans hold their collective breath, ready to roar their approval. The entire stadium waits to hear the starting whistle and see the opening kickoff. It cleanses the palette and clears the air!

My kickoff was no less dramatic as it signaled the beginning of the most important journey of my life. It was the reason I was born, and what I was meant to do. Like an ancient Japanese Blacksmith creating a samurai sword, my destiny began like a piece of iron being forged into steel. It began with fire. A heat so hot, it created a fire and sharpened an edge I still feel to this day.

"When I feel the heat, I see the light." Everett Dirksen

Far from home and in a strange setting, my return to my

"Football Life" began in the peculiar way and with some very odd people. It was a training camp like no other I had ever experienced. Each day was long, hard and hot. The more I did, the farther away "making the team" seemed to get.

This particular day the class had been over for hours, but the room, still hot and humid, is hovering at about 95 degrees. The cantaloupe colored carpet is sweat soaked, body stench stained and we are sitting in the middle of it.

The place is Los Angeles, and it is Hot Yoga Guru, Bikram Choudhury's Fall 2003 Teacher Training. Sitting on the floor, we are leaning against our purple floor chairs called back-jacks waiting for the evening lecture to begin. It's the middle of week five of a nine week, 700 hour, yoga teacher training course. The experienced teachers know that week five is "hell week." It's a time when even the strongest student-trainees start to crack. Never mind that the weaker ones, who since the beginning, have been spinning out of control.

This is the hardest, physically and mentally draining test I have ever been involved in. Twice daily workouts in 120-degree heat, with 300 souls stuffed into a room designed for 200. Sixteen-hour days are average, with endless lectures, constant demands, and a new torture invention called a "dialogue clinic." The Marine Corps would be proud to adopt this training for their new recruits!

Just a few weeks before, we were en-route from our Canadian home. My trip down the California coastline with my girlfriend, Erica, was filled with conversation and anticipation. She looked up from a paper she was memorizing and asked, "Aren't you going to study the dialogue?"

"Study the dialogue? Hell ... I'm paying 10,000 bucks for this course. They can teach me!" was my cocky, tongue-in-cheek response. Although I enjoyed being funny, there was a lot of truth in my statement.

Erica smiled a knowing smile, saying, "I think you'd better look at this." I credit her as the inspiration for this experience and ultimately, for me discovering my true self. I'd been teaching Karate professionally for over 25 years, during which I had done a lot of public speaking. I was confident with my ability to perform under pressure and to get up in front of people. The hidden fact was, I had never really memorized anything before, except perhaps the times tables. Even at that, I could only get to about 8 X 8 before I faltered. Besides, I knew the basic idea of what was going on there, so I'd figure it out as it happened.

Week five was something else. Everyone was sore, tired, sleep deprived, and completely frazzled. It was routine for people to throw up, faint, or just plain lay down from exhaustion during classes. Many peoples' systems had shut down from sweating, as they had leached the minerals out of their bodies. An ambulance had shown up on three occasions, twice to take someone away as a result of dehydration, and once for an epileptic seizure gone bad.

The person who suffered the seizure was dismissed immediately and deemed unfit to be a teacher. The message was clear from the first day Bikram said, "If you want to quit, you can have your money back right now - today. Tomorrow, we start our first class. No refunds!" Then with fiery eyes and a big smile he finished, "Besides, I have already eaten your money!"

The next day he turned up the heat and stretched the 90-minute class into a 2½-hour marathon. My God, I thought I was going to die ... and that was only the beginning on this, our very first day!

God, it was hot! Forget about frying an egg on the sidewalk! This kind of heat would fry an egg inside the chicken!

Mentally, the pressure cooker was the document known as the dialogue. The dialogue was a fifty-page manuscript that had to be memorized and performed, verbatim, by every student. Any mistakes or words out of place would give you a failing grade. For Bikram, there was no room for ad-libbing and no tolerance for anything other than what was on the written page. The curriculum teachers marked our every flaw as they graded pace, voice control, and presence. The crowning glory was, not only did you have to perform in front of the entire class, but it was mandatory that you listen to every other person perform each part of the dialogue. There were hours upon hours of endless sitting and listening to people struggle with the scripted words.

You waited your turn, hoping to get the words right in your head, by nervously mumbling along with the person speaking. Some trainees were professional actors and singers who said this was the toughest thing they had ever seen. Of the 300 student-trainees, there were ten who were failing, and I was one of the worst. I was in deep, deep trouble.

"Having doesn't mean anything! Having doesn't mean anything, if you don't know how to use it!" bellowed Bikram from his elevated podium. He sat like a king in his leather chair surveying his minions.

I have met many unusual characters during my time as a Martial Artist, but I have to say Yogi/Guru Bikram topped the list. His eccentric, Napoleonic presence was bigger than life. It wasn't until you got close to him that you realized just how small of a man he was. I had him at 60 yrs. old, about 5'2, and "a buck twenty soaking wet." He was fit and strong, with a baldhead and a long black ponytail hanging down his back.

He sported a gold Rolex watch and was almost naked save for his small, black Speedo swimsuit, which he called his costume.

Fluent in many languages, Bikram, with his Indian accent, swore like a sailor, talked like a biker, and acted like a gangster. He boasted of sleeping only two hours per night and eating only half of a ham sandwich per day. Everything he did was exaggerated. Craziness aside, he would transform into a guru as he imparted the wisdom of the sutras and taught his yoga. You either loved him or hated him. We decided to love him.

"You people here in America ... having doesn't mean anything, if you don't know how to use it. You have everything here. All the money, all the wealth, all the cars and homes, but you are the unhappiest people in the world," he preached. "I come from Calcutta. There, the people have nothing, just poverty - barely the clothes on their back, but they are the happiest," was his insightful evening lecture.

"Now I live in Beverly Hills. You know, I have the largest swimming pool in Hollywood, and it's quarter of a mile long!" he said proudly, "but I don't know how to swim! You see, having doesn't mean anything, if you don't know how to use it."

"The swimming pool has no value to me in my life. It's like trying to start a Mercedes Benz car with a Toyota key. It doesn't work. You Americans have everything but you are the most bankrupt people in the world. Can you stand straight; can you lock your knee? You have a body, a mind, and a soul, but you don't know how to use them," he continued.

Bikram could talk for hours and never lose a beat. He enjoyed keeping you up until 1:00 or 2:00 am, knowing that you had to be back to yoga class at 9:00 am.

"You have no peace, dumb fucks! Your problem is that you have no real problems. Your first problem in life was when you met me and you came into the hot room. You look in the mirror and see your fat belly and you see yourself for the first time!" he taunted.

"Well, we've got problems now!" I thought - still no end in sight and another month in this mad house.

I had a whole list of reasonable excuses, like "I only came to support Erica. I didn't care about being a yoga teacher, or the yoga was not a passion for me." Yet here I was in the middle of this thing, emotionally stripped and with no control.

At the end of week five Bikram held a mid-term test. He and his panel of instructors would help the people who were failing by giving them an extra chance to perform. It was a mandatory opportunity to get upgraded to a passing mark.

I figured this was my chance to have my natural "get it done" talent come alive. I could redeem myself right here by seizing the moment and acing it. It was not easy. Once we had finished presenting, Bikram's number one, Craig Villiani, announced the names of those with passing grades. Mueller was not one of them.

On the walk back, Craig took me aside and said, "A heads up for you ... Bikram says that no matter how well you improve in the final weeks, you will have to perform the final test. Don't know why dude, just thought you should know." The final test was reserved as a last chance on the last day of training for the worst of the worst to make the grade. It also meant constant and continued anxiety. So there it was 100% reality, all truth, and no hope.

It was true, I didn't care much about being a yoga teacher, but I don't like to fail. Since I had no choice, I would give it my best shot. If it was not good enough for Bikram, then screw him, that was his problem.

In addition to all the regular dialogue practice we were doing during the day, I began getting up early, at 6:00 a.m., to recite for an additional 45 minutes. I might fail, but I wasn't going down without a fight. Over the final few weeks Bikram increased the pressure, wearing us out even more as he kept us later and later with his evening lectures.

I can't say that my ability to recite the dialogue improved much, but on the final day I did receive a probationary pass for the effort. It was an ordeal I would not care to repeat. That said, I would recommend this training to anyone. I have been to many "self-help" seminars, but never anything as gut wrenching as this. Perhaps it was the intense yoga, or the pressure, or both.

Maybe it was Bikram's iron fisted approach, working his yoga with a true eastern discipline. I'm not sure why the course of nine weeks in Bikram's torture chamber was so profound, but it was. Most of the trainees felt it, but I doubt many as deeply as I did.

On reflection, I realized that for the first time in my life, my personality had not helped me. At this training, who you were, how you were, or what you were did not matter. Nobody cared.

Bob's B.S.
Don't leave the room, just deal with your shit - here and now.

Regardless of any perceived injury, complaint, or problem you may have, the answer was always the same. No problem, just go back into the hot room and do the yoga.

Hell, a young woman got the news that her father had died unexpectedly of a heart attack. She was begrudgingly given the weekend off to attend the funeral. When she returned, she had to make up the missed time by doing triple classes. No problem was accepted. The consistent yoga message was - go back into the hot room and deal with it.

With the hardship came an epiphany.

I had always been the likeable kid who tried hard, but perhaps I held back a little. Perhaps I held back a lot! My happy personality and easy demeanor had always gained favor with my teachers, coaches, and business associates. That is, until Bikram. For the first time in my life, being a good guy didn't matter. In fact, it was worth nothing.

"Having doesn't mean anything, if you don't know how to use it."

> ### Bob's B.S.
> I realized that throughout my entire life someone had always shown up to help me. I had always been saved when things had gotten tough or when I might fail.

Be it a teacher, a friend, or even a lucky circumstance, someone or something had always stepped up to help me. Many times I'd received a pass I didn't deserve. I remember not liking it, but I took it with the promise to be better next time.

I had tried to get a pass with Bikram by using my special skills, my force of will, and my natural talent. No one cared who or what I was. It just didn't matter here.

"Can you lock the knee? Can you do the yoga? Do you see your real self in the mirror? Problems, you have no problems. Just go back in the hot room and deal with it. Your life is about discovering your s-e-l-f. Nothing else matters."

Without a shadow of a doubt, nine weeks of suffering in Bikram's torture chamber was one of the most profound experiences ever. Within a few months of returning home, my life would be changed forever.

A series of synchronistic events were about to begin as I looked in the mirror and asked myself:

"What do I have that I am not using? What do I want"

Take-away

Obstacles are opportunities in disguise.
When you have a problem don't look for a way out look for
a way through.
What do you have that you are not using?
What do you want?

51% Dreaming

The Second Quarter

Typically the second quarter is about the "game plan." You find out who, and what you have prepared for. With the first quarter jitters and mistakes gone, you now get to see if your game plan works. Created from your playbook, your plan is tested, both by you and your opponent.

Now the history of where you have been and what you have done before is helpful. As you execute your preconceived plan you'll find the need to be open to the possibilities of the game. No amount of planning can prepare you for the unexpected and when it happens you have to be ready to act. What do you do when an opportunity creates an opening? What's in your playbook? My Sensei once taught, "You'll learn how to fight when you give your opponent your best shot and they just look at you like it was nothing!"

"The two most important days in your life are the day you are born and the day you find out why." – Mark Twain

While I don't remember being born, I do remember the day I asked a question and discovered my why. Then I found myself in an art store asking more questions.

"I used to be an artist when I was a kid and I would like to paint. Can you tell me what I need to get started?" I asked. The clerk at the Opus art store looked at me with a smile and immediately began to load me up with all the essentials. I left the store an hour later, full of ambition and with my wallet $600 lighter. I had bought everything. All the paints, brushes, and canvas I might need, plus a "How To" book about painting. It was January. It was a new year, and I, at 48 years old, was excited about art again. I was going home to paint a portrait of an old friend who had just come back into my life.

A few weeks before, on an empty afternoon, I was staring at a blank computer screen. Erica had gone to Calgary for the weekend to visit her daughter. It was my second day without her, and I was scratching around for something to do. I had watched all the TV humanly possible, now I was sitting motionless before the silent keyboard, looking for inspiration. This was one of my first ever internet-surfing sessions. When the word EBAY came into my mind, I clicked on the homepage that quickly filled the screen. A small empty box appeared with the word "search" beside it. Looking at the empty search box I imagined it to say, "What are you interested in? What do you want?"

My eyes rolled up and as I looked skyward I asked myself, "What am I interested in? What do I want?" Immediately, without thinking, I blurted out,

"I'M INTERESTED IN DICK BUTKUS!"

The thought transported me back to my hometown of Victoria B.C. and the Hornets logo on a large sign at the entrance to Glanford field. The gridiron at the park was packed with young boys. It was try out day for the 1969 Junior

Bantam Saanich Hornets. I was among 150 kids running, doing calisthenics, and learning agility drills on the hardpan clay and grass field.

The coaches were lead by a six foot five, square jawed man in his mid twenties. Roy Vollinger was a character with a boisterously loud voice, lots of brass, and an absolute maniacal love for football. At first, I was a little afraid of him. He had a big, commanding presence, but you quickly felt his warm heart and his passion for teaching football. He oversaw the assistant coaches and all the potential players with a watchful, educated eye. At the end of the day, I was among the 40 kids he had chosen to come back the next week for a second look.

I was big for my age, athletic, and I really wanted to play football. At 12, I was one of the youngest kids chosen, but also one of the biggest and quickest rookies to make the team. After the second week, we got our pads and our helmets and once outfitted, we felt like real football players. The lineman shoulder pads were oversized and when you put your helmet on, you felt invincible. I would come to love the smell of the fresh grass and enjoy the mud that stained our uniforms.

For the next five seasons our team won the championship each year and, in 1972, like the Miami Dolphins, we were undefeated. The reason was simple. Our coach worked us hard. We practiced three to four times per week, three hours per night. You could count on practice being 30 minutes longer than scheduled, as he would want extra wind sprints and grass drills at the end. Playing for a winning team like the Saanich Hornets was my first experience with becoming a disciplined athlete. I worked hard to simply be good at my assignment, and became a winner because of that effort. This created a foundation for success that I used later on in my martial arts training and in my business. As part of this great experience, the team would have movie nights once or twice per season. During our second season the coach showed a special film. I had never seen Dick Butkus in action, so I was dumbfounded when the 1969 film about the "most feared man in football" was played at our clubhouse. Everything about Butkus amazed me. It was all out devastation when he tackled or hit someone. He was always around the ball and made a routine play look incredible. He seemingly controlled the entire field. That was it - I wanted to be Dick Butkus!

Bob's B.S.
Vollinger regularly invoked Dick Butkus and the number 51 during practices. He told us, Butkus was the best - a true player that nobody could beat.

Most memorable was his menacing image, the middle linebacker stance, and his pigeon toed, lumbering walk. He was John Wayne in cleats! He gave me chills and it inspired me!

At about the same time, the movie, "Brian's Song," premiered on TV. It was the 1971 Emmy award-winning story about the football friendship of Gale Sayers and Brian Piccolo. It told of how two complete opposites, one black/ one white, one talented/one not, faced challenges. How they came together as Piccolo was stricken down, fighting against lung cancer. With the image of a larger than life Butkus dominating on the field and the passion I felt from "Brian's Song," I became a Chicago Bears fan for life.

As an outlet for my passion, I began creating charcoal football drawings. My work quickly made me the top artist in junior high. The art teacher, Mr. Bowes, recognized my talent right away and encouraged me to draw what inspired me. He was an odd, but a very special teacher and he encouraged me to develop my natural talent. He gave me the materials, his time, and most importantly, his praise. It was the kind of support I craved, and I responded by growing my talent. I worked hard, re-creating the Dick Butkus image that I admired. I made large and small portraits, sometimes drawing the same image over and over again.

I also created artwork of players like Gale Sayers, Kareem Abdul-Jabbar, and many others. Given my age, I was also newly fascinated with the female form, so I began to draw girls from my dad's Playboy magazines. Drawing the beautiful girls quickly rivaled my football work, and those pictures really got noticed. The pieces were so well received that, by grade ten, I sold most of them to the male teachers.

Thus began a magical time for me. For two years I spent most of my school time in the art room. Practicing and playing football consumed my evenings, and all my spare time was spent drawing in my bedroom. I imagined I would be a great professional football player someday, and perhaps a world famous artist.

Going into grade eleven, things began to change dramatically. A few seasons ago I had been one of the bigger kids on the team, but since then, I had not grown. As our team progressed through the Bantam league and into the Junior and College ranks, many of us started to fall away. I lacked the finesse and skills to play other positions and playing on the line became tougher and tougher. To quote an old football joke, "His lack of size is only compensated for by his lack of speed!"

At the same time, my artwork faced a challenge. I had moved to a new school and a new art teacher who didn't approve of realistic drawings in general and specifically, didn't like my football work. He wanted free form ideas and more abstract renditions, but that didn't interest me. The more I resisted, the less encouragement he offered, and I soon lost interest in my art.

My "coming of age" was now in full bloom, as I discovered girls and alcohol. Everything else fell by the wayside as I immersed myself in teenage fun. Like most things I wanted to do, once I started, I was all in. I got to hang out with a faster, more experienced crowd because I looked older than my age. The more I enjoyed the parties and my friends, the less I wanted to deal with the difficulties at football and the challenges to my art. This influenced me, as all my older friends were graduating or leaving school, and I wanted to join them.

By the end of grade eleven I quit football, I quit art, and then I quit school. I had lost interest in my childhood. It was time to move on. I left home at age sixteen, off to seek my fortune. I left the kid stuff, the art, the dreams and I grew up fast. Although I didn't know it at the time, 1973 was also Dick Butkus's last year in football. His bad knees caused him to retire early. That year, he too, quit the game he loved.

It took thirty-one years, two careers, and a lifetime of alternate experiences for me to rediscover my passion and my true talent. Motivational expert, Tony Robbins says, "You can change your mind, your mood, and your life in a moment. All you have to do is ask the right question." When my unconscious mind heard the question, "What do I want?" my super-conscious offered me both a hidden passion and a forgotten hero.

I said out loud, "Ya, I'm interested in Dick Butkus!"

I typed his name and instantly 800 items appeared on my computer screen. For the next five hours I searched through each Dick Butkus piece, reveling in the experience. I was like a kid in a candy store. It's difficult to express the sense of pure joy that I felt that afternoon. I had rediscovered my boyhood hero and was transported back to being a young man on a grass field. I immediately began to purchase jerseys, footballs, memorabilia, and old sports magazines. If I found an item between the Butkus playing years of 1965 to 1973, I would buy it.

All this led up to the morning I received a copy of an old magazine. Over 30 years ago, as a kid, I had owned this 1970 edition of Sports Illustrated. On the cover was Dick Butkus, number 51, looking particularly upset and the caption underneath the photo read, "The most feared man in football." There it was that same feeling, rich and full. Like a child, I savored it, relished every word and every picture. Inside the magazine was a photo of Butkus charging forward in full flight. Now, for the second time in my life, I was artistically inspired by Butkus, inspired enough to take action.

When I arrived home from the Opus Art store, I proudly showed Erica all my art stuff. I quickly thumbed through the art book, looking at the pictures. Within a few minutes I put it down, thinking it was too complicated to read. With that decision, I handed it to her and said, "Here, you can read this if you want to. I'm going to get started."

This was the beginning of 18 months of absorbed focus, an almost maniacal effort painting Dick Butkus. I studied every detail I could find about him and his career. New items would arrive from EBay every week with more pictures and images for me to analyze as potential projects.

I would later describe the experience as being like the Steven Spielberg movie, "Close Encounters of the Third Kind." The main character, played by Richard Dreyfess, becomes obsessed with an image of a mountain. At the apex of his obsession he dumps a bowl of mashed potatoes on the kitchen table and starts molding the image that is in his mind. That's exactly how I felt about Butkus.

I didn't know why and I didn't care why. I just knew I had to do this. I loved telling people about Dick Butkus. I would say his name and enjoy the reaction that came along with it. I was delighted, although somewhat surprised by just how many people had heard of him, including women. They might not know who or what he was, but they knew the name. I would hear everything from, "What the heck is a Dick Butkus?" to "Ya, Butkus. That guy was something else!"

If anyone showed any interest at all - I mean, even a hint, out came my stuff. The "refrigerator art" is what I call it. Do you remember yourself as a 5 year old? And, what your mother did with any art or writing you created? Then you'll know what I am talking about. I would show people my paintings and while I was pleased with the compliments, I didn't have any plans for the painting. It seemed to be more than a hobby, but I can't say that I saw any purpose to it. I just enjoyed the fun of it and how good it made me feel. Whatever door had opened from the yoga experience was not for me to figure out. I was having way too much fun just running with it.

Along the way I tried painting other things, people, and scenery, but nothing satisfied me like painting Butkus. As I continued painting, I felt the need to do more. I started developing a karate seminar and lecture for the various dojos that I led. I would put on a #51 jersey and teach karate techniques that I thought were similar to football. Then, at the end of the event, I would tell the students my story about becoming an artist and following my dreams. I figured it was a good story and an even better message to teach kids and adults.

"Follow your dreams, and then let them lead you," was my motto. I enjoyed making fun of my obsession for Dick Butkus, but what I really liked was getting people inspired. Next to painting, having an audience and telling stories was my favorite thing to do.

At the end of one of these lectures, a senior student, Don Lovell, approached me in a formal manner. Don, a few years older than me was very clean-cut, army lean, and wiry. Ex-military, he was extremely respectful, but also forthright and always to the point. I enjoyed him, as he always brought his gung-ho, army readiness to the dojo. He was respected by his peers and by his teachers, including me.

He stood in front of me with a "Permission to speak?" look on his face. "Sensei, I truly enjoyed your talk this evening. Thank you. I found it, and your art, very inspiring," he said. "I wondered if I could suggest my take on it for you."

I knew if Don had something to say, it would usually be well thought out and rehearsed. This, however, was somewhat impromptu for him. He did not leave things to chance nor did he mince words, so I was immediately interested in his observations.

"Sensei, you made me interested in football, even though I am not. When you talk about Dick Butkus, you create so much energy. It is amazing! However, I heard something in your description that I think you should know." He took a breath and then said, "You talk about Butkus as a person, but what I hear is more an adjective or a metaphor of sorts. Have you ever thought of him as a verb, as opposed to a noun? Like "a Butkus" was an objective or a tool, not just a person?" he asked.

A verb and an action, rather than static object or person… what an interesting thought? How fitting, movement and action! This struck me as being quite profound, although I can't say I got it right away. Don continued, "You see, by admiring Dick Butkus you found your passion for your art.

Bob's B.S.
No disrespect to Mr. Butkus, but I see a "Butkus" as a thing, not just as a person. You found your art when you found your Butkus!"

"Finding Your Butkus" was born at that moment by a keen observation from a clever student. Not only was this an "a-ha moment" for me personally, but now it was a quest with a future. I had only seen my passion for Butkus as the past joy that it was, but Don's perception gave it a renewed sense of what it could be.

Bob's B.S.
"Finding Your Butkus" wasn't about celebrating the past. It was more about creating action for the future.

Dick Butkus was endless movement on the field, roaming, scrapping, and then dynamically striking. All 245 pounds of him delivered the tackling blow, like no player before or since.

This had all happened for a reason.

"WHAT DO YOU WANT?" was the question I had asked myself and this had been my answer. I would take all my experience and combine it with all my talent and drive to be the person I had always dreamed of being. I would be an artist, and I would strive to be an artist of life.

The future would have synergistic events happening one after another. Each event, good or bad, would challenge my self-belief beyond what I thought possible. I would meet Dick Butkus personally, develop my art and creativity, and tell my story to a bigger audience. A much, much bigger audience! I would do things and go places that I could never have imagined or dreamed of.

Bob's B.S.
Years ago, I could not have imagined that the daydreams of a little boy would become so important to a man's life.

""Finding Your Butkus"" became a story about finding your true self and then taking action. But they were, and this was just the beginning, again.

Take-away

Your childhood may hold a secret ambition or key that can unlock success for you. What is it?
Do your have a personal hero?
What qualities make up your idea of a hero?
What is your special talent and how might it apply to the hero?
What action can you take to use the qualities you admire and make them your own?

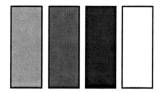

Print the Legend

Meeting Dick Butkus

The Third Quarter

The third quarter always follows the half time break. After the marching bands and the cheerleaders have left the field; the teams are ready to finish the game. Now is about control, "ball control". There isn't the same kind of mystery like before. The first half either proved your game-plan to be sound or it revealed its weakness. Regardless of your success to date, now it's time to adjust your game plan and take control.

This is the quarter where your will power, your ability, and your circumstance all come together to set the table for success. The ancient Chinese Philosopher, General Sun Tzu says, "If you only know your enemy you will succeed 50% of the time. Like wise if you only know yourself you will succeed 50% of the time. But if you know yourself and your opponent you will win 100%, every time."

The third quarter measures the knowledge you have acquired and turns it into potential wisdom. My third quarter followed a first half of huge learning, combined with tremendous growth and potential success. My game plan now developed, I sought to soar and attain what, just a few years before, was unthinkable!

The question was, did I have the balls to do it?

"This is the west, Sir. When the fact becomes a legend, print the legend," said the newsman to Jimmy Stewart in the 1962 movie, "The Man Who Shot Liberty Valance."

When the elevator doors opened, the 22nd floor was actually a combination of two complete levels. The structure was an impressive expanse of tall ceilings and a long winding staircase that led to the conference rooms and offices. Erica and I were at 10100 Santa Monica Blvd, on the top floor, overlooking the sprawling city of Los Angeles. This was the lobby of the biggest law firm either of us had ever seen, and we were here to meet Mr. Fred Richman.

As he approached, Fred looked to be about 70 years old, with bushy eyebrows and a warm smile. We both liked him right away. As we followed him into his office, he apologized for the mess and quickly shoved a couple of stacks of files and papers to one side of his desk. There were piles of paper everywhere, along with some family photos, a fishing picture, and a bronze statue. The trophy immediately caught my eye. I recognized the special figure on the upper shelf, and remembered the phone call that I'd received a couple of months earlier.

Outside the door of our Kelowna condo, I could hear the phone ringing. I quickly unlocked the door, threw my sweaty yoga shorts and towels on the floor, and ran to answer the call by the third ring.

"Hello", I puffed with a short breath.

"Is this Bob Mueller?" asked the voice.

"Yes," I puffed again.

"It's Fred Richman from Leob & Leob," said the voice. "Dick Butkus's lawyer. We received your FAX and Dick likes your work!"

"Dick ... who?" I stammered, as I tried to catch myself. "Dick Butkus? THE Dick Butkus likes my work!?"

"Yes, that's right and ..." the voice continued.

I heard nothing. I don't remember how long the conversation was and I don't remember what was said. All I heard was "Dick likes your work" then my mind went blank as I was overcome with joy! As soon as I hung up the phone I started yelling, "Whooop, whoop, wow, wow, wow!" I then marched around the condo, breathing heavily and smiling ear to ear. If you are supposed to live in the moment, I was! This was the sweet thrill of an unexpected, but highly anticipated moment. I started calling anyone I could think of. It was only 11:00 a.m. Although I didn't connect with many people, I know that I overwhelmed a few people with my excitement. This was a moment I had thought about many times before but hadn't really prepared myself for. Now that it was here, I was ready to step into the next stage of my adventure.

Late that afternoon I called Fred Richman back and admitted that I didn't remember much of our earlier conversation. He laughed, and told me what the next step would be.

I did remember I'd recently had a chance meeting with Mark Yarnell outside his favorite restaurant. Mark was a legendary network-marketing expert whom I'd become friends with a few years before. Yarnell speaks with an American twang, born of his Missouri upbringing and his Texas life style. His clear blue eyes shine perpetually with excitement, and his quick mind and sharp wit had made him a world famous celebrity. During the 1980's he'd lived a classic rags to riches story. He went from being a bankrupt Texas preacher in a small oil town, to becoming a multi-millionaire within a few years. After earning a fortune with a company called Nuskin International, he became a best selling author and a professional speaker. His story is the kind that fuels dreams, and his passion for life inspires anyone who is fortunate enough to hear him speak.

We became friends when he moved from Reno, Nevada to Victoria, British Columbia and now fate had us both living in Kelowna B.C. I enjoyed and learned a great deal from Mark whenever I had the opportunity to spend time with him. He was always bursting with ideas and developing strategies to implement them.

"What's happening Bobbo?" Mark twanged with a big grin. "How's them Dick Butkus cards doing?"

I was always happy to see Mark, as his tremendous energy is contagious. "Things are good," I replied. "But I'm not having much luck contacting Butkus. I've sent Fed Ex packages to his home, the NFL Hall of Fame and I've called everywhere I can think of, but no luck yet," I lamented. "I even called his lawyer in L.A. and boy, that was the shortest conversation ever. The lawyer was abrupt and just said to send a FAX!"

"Hell, with your talent, I'd have thought you'd be in business already," Mark encouraged. "Men's greeting cards are a frontier market, with no competition. There's nothing anywhere for men and you could bust it wide open with those Tough Guy Cards!"

Mark was the one who first suggested the idea of creating men's greeting cards. We had met for lunch the spring before when I discussed my new passion for painting and then showed him some of my artwork. After looking at the paintings he reminisced about his favorite football story of how Dick Butkus had dreamed of hitting someone so hard that their head, along with their helmet, went flying off! Then he laughed, "That's one mean sum-bitch!"

He looked at the paintings again and said, "I've had a business idea rolling around in my head for over twenty years and you can have it if you want." He then put his hands up to gesture a square type motion, dramatically saying, "Men's greeting cards! You know, there isn't anything, anywhere in the market place. When I look at your art, that's what I see. I see men's greeting cards!"

He added, "I know a few football players, like Danny White of the Cowboys and the old Pittsburgh Steelers running back, Rocky Bleier. If you want, I could put you in contact with them."

I declined, as Butkus was my only focus, but the card idea really got me excited.

It was Mark's idea that was the spark, not just for the cards, but also for my confidence to try to meet Dick Butkus. Up to this point I had been painting Butkus' image just for the pure joy of it. I had dreamed about him seeing a painting some day and then signing it. However, until "Tough Guy" cards were born, it was just that, a daydream.

The lunch with Mark Yarnell created a renewed burst of mad energy. I began creating new works of art and designing a unique line of greeting cards for men. The concept looked professional right away and I was confident that it was a product with huge market potential.

Things moved rapidly until it came time to actually get the material in front of Dick Butkus. I had never done anything like this before. In truth, I'd never had to research or find anything or anybody. This project proved to be very different. I tried many things, such as writing letters, making internet connections, and chasing down addresses. I even traveled to Chicago to attend a sports memorabilia show. Butkus was featured as one of the top attractions, but he had to pull out at the last minute for some unknown reason. I attended anyway and brought my son, Leigh, with me. Together we saw our first live Bears game at Soldier Field. It was 2005 and the Chicago Bears met the Indianapolis Colts in a mismatch.

After the game we had dinner at Mike Ditka's Bar. We were seated beside a large round table full of exceptionally big men. As we received our menus, Leigh recognized Peyton Manning, the famed quarterback of the Colts, as the man heading the round table. He was sitting with five or six huge guys, who we guessed were his offensive line. They were celebrating the 41 to 10 whipping they had given the Bears earlier that day.

A number of people went up to his table and interrupted Manning to get an autograph. Although we wanted to, being polite Canadians, we were too chicken to approach him. Of course being chicken or simply polite is a matter of your point of view.

Points of view were the central issue when John Wayne asked, "Pilgrim, where do you think you're going?" as he questioned James Stewart.

Jimmy Stewart was joined by "the Duke" and Lee Marvin to make John Ford's 1962 morality tale called, 'The Man Who Shot Liberty Valance." The story has a frontier, greenhorn lawyer named Randsom Stoddart, (Jimmy Stewart), who is begrudgingly befriended by a tough guy gunfighter, Tom

Donovan, (John Wayne). Together they are pitted against Liberty Valance, (Lee Marvin); one of the silver screen's all time best villains.

Jimmy Stewart is the underdog, and is tormented by the bully, Lee Marvin. He is humiliated and goaded into a gunfight he cannot possibly survive. However, honor dictates he must fight and, by some twist of fate, he survives the duel, killing Liberty Valance. He and his story become a legend, thus making him a hero. Then he gets the girl and becomes a famous leader in the community. What Stoddart doesn't know is he has had a guardian angel, John Wayne. The Duke's character, Tom Donovan, is a man who reluctantly sacrifices his love for the girl and his own morals to come to the aid of the underdog. He secretly and simultaneously shoots Liberty Valance himself, but leaves Randsom Stoddart thinking it is he who has actually killed the antagonist. Later, upon hearing the truth, Stoddart has to live with the fact that he did not do what he has been rewarded for.

The movie is one of my all time favorites. The story tells about truth. More importantly, it is the complicated perception of truth. All the characters struggle to be true to their beliefs and their collective conscience. I love the movie's underdog character and his multi-layered struggle to overcome his demons.

Standing in front of Mark, I found myself confessing my fears and my frustration. "I don't know how this is going to happen." I said out loud, letting out a sigh of doubt for the first time. "Mark, I don't know if I will be able to get this in front of Butkus, but I do think that the "Tough Guy" cards are for real. Maybe I should shift directions and get Rocky's number from you. Maybe I'll try the cards out on him."

"Don't worry about how it will happen. All you have to

do is want it," Yarnell reminded me. He agreed to get Bleire's phone number later in the day and told me to give him a call on Friday morning. It was a call I never made.

Now Erica and I were sitting in an expensive Los Angeles lawyer's office. I was staring at a real "Butkus Award" Trophy, while Fred was telling Dick Butkus stories. Mr. Butkus was supposed to be there, but a family emergency had him go to Florida, as one of his older brothers was having open-heart surgery. I had missed him again! Fred Richman explained that family was very important to Dick and he offered his apologies for his missing client.

"Dick likes your work and he would like to know a little more about how you see marketing these cards," Fred asked, but before I could answer he went further into telling his stories. He spoke about how he, like Butkus, was an Illinois graduate. He had been a senior when Dick's football prowess led the Illinois football team to a victory at the 1963 Rose Bowl. I thought it was great and I could have listened all day. He talked more about how Dick had done very well after football, but in truth, all he had was his good name. It was Fred's job to protect it. He wouldn't let anyone coattail on the Dick Butkus franchise, not without his proper due-diligence.

"Dick is a great guy, very funny, with a great sense of humor," Fred said. "But he is not quick to befriend people and he is quite conservative when you first meet him."   He continued, "One time I got a call from a guy who wanted to pay Butkus to play golf with him. To put him off, I told him that Dick's standard fee was $25,000 for a personal appearance. You know, the guy still wanted to do it and he was willing to pay the 25 grand for

18 holes! But I knew that Dick wouldn't be keen on it, so I told the guy that I could probably get Dick to play with him, but couldn't guarantee that Dick would actually talk to him. You know, if it struck him the wrong way, Dick wouldn't have said a word to that guy, even through a whole game of golf." Fred's eyes lit up saying, "And when he's working, or on a movie set, he can get himself into a mind set where he doesn't like any distractions at all! It's that same focus that made him such a great player and sometimes it's not very nice," Fred concluded.

It was Erica who reminded both of us that we were here to talk about the cards, at least a little. She asked about the kind of backing and support that would happen when Mr. Butkus approved a product. What were their expectations? What did they need from us? I, on the other hand, was reveling in the experience, and still keeping one eye on the Butkus Award sitting on the upper shelf.

"As I told you on the phone, Dick is not interested in being your partner, but he will support a product, when it gets closer to being in the marketplace," Fred explained. With that, he looked at the full color samples in my portfolio and he liked what he saw. Until now, all he had seen were a couple of black and white sample images via the FAX machine.

Looking at his watch, Fred began to wind down the meeting. "Bob, I'm very impressed with this and I believe that we can get behind these cards. I do recommend however, that you make some larger samples. It would make a better presentation," he offered. He then picked up his phone and began to dial. "Dick, Fred Richman here," speaking into the receiver "I'm sitting here with Bob and Erica Mueller, regarding the 'Tough Guy Cards.' I like what I see so, subject to your approval, I suggest that we support the further development of this. Call me back when you get the message."

As we got up to leave, I started to motion toward the trophy. "I was wondering when you were going to ask," smiled Fred. "Here, let me get it down for you." The next moment Erica was snapping a picture of me holding the trophy for Collegiate Linebacker of the Year, "The Butkus Award." I was in hog heaven. Full of confidence now, I closed the meeting with, "Mr. Richman, I want these cards to be so successful that Dick Butkus will be remembered as much for "Touch Guy" cards as he is for being a Chicago Bear!"

On the way back to our Hollywood motel, we talked about our great meeting. Fred Richman had said Dick Butkus owned the rights to his image, as he had retired before the league had banned such rights. It all sounded good and I was sure that my cards would be on the shelves right away! I had accomplished an impossible goal. Dick Butkus knew who I was, liked my work, and now was prepared to endorse it. I envisioned a rack of "Tough Guy" cards in every store in America and soon ... we would be rich!

Spring turned to summer and as the months passed I began to learn about the strangle-hold the NFL (and in fact all professional sports leagues) have on licensed products. Fred introduced me to a marketing expert named Bob Sgarlata. Bob was a consultant who had been the Vice-President of Marketing for Walgreen's for many years. His specialty was in greeting cards and he had put together many deals for superstar clients such as Gale Sayers, Michael Jordan, and Tiger Woods. I believed he soon would be putting a deal together with me.

Right from the start, Bob said he was doing this as a favor for his friend, Dick Butkus. He promised he would be straight forward and 100% honest in his appraisal. If he didn't like what he saw or didn't think it could work, he wouldn't waste his time or mine. Fortunately, he was impressed with my cards, but warned me of the rocky road to success with this kind of venture. Too many good products never make it to market due to licensing and royalty problems. To further complicate things, even if we got the NFL on side and could pay their fees, then we would need each and every individual player to agree to the product. Of course everyone in the "food chain" would have a say and receive a piece of the royalty. I was starting to understand why there was no competition in the marketplace for men's greeting cards.

By the end of the summer I was scheduling an extra trip to Toronto. Every May, I was required to attend a Black Belt Grading back East. This year there were additional students ready for their Black Belt test, so an extra grading in Toronto was needed. Sensei Scott Bullard, one of my original students from the Brockville days, had created a very successful Canada's Best Karate School in Woodbridge, Ontario. In fact, he surpassed my accomplishments on many levels, making his school the best in our group. As the leader of CBK Inc., it was my job to test his brown belt students for the rank of Black Belt.

As I was making my travel arrangements for the grading I heard that Dick Butkus was making a new ESPN reality TV series called "Bound for Glory." The show was being shot on location, in a little place called McKee's Rocks, just outside of Pittsburgh, PA. This sounded interesting! It was a 317.5-mile drive from Toronto. If I rented a car, I could be there in five or six hours. I made some calls, altered my plans, and set up the meeting I had been dreaming of all my life.

The husky, U.S. customs officer at the Niagara Falls border crossing asked, "Where are you going?"

With a big grin, I handed him one of my new Butkus Collection "Tough Guy" business cards and said, "I'm going to see a guy named Dick Butkus."

"THE Dick Butkus?" he questioned, as his face softened and his eyes widened. I had come to realize if I was talking to an American male over the age of thirty, the name Dick Butkus was a guaranteed door opener. This border guard was no exception.

"Yes, THE Dick Butkus," I smiled again. For the next few minutes we held up traffic as he told how he was a big Buffalo Bills fan, but Dick Butkus was the man. "That guy was the best ever," he gushed, and we both enjoyed our mutual admiration moment.

It was about 7:00 p.m, with the sun starting to set. My plan was to get across the border, drive for an hour or so, and find a cheapie motel that had a TV with ESPN 2. The next day I would be well rested and would finish my drive to Pittsburgh.

Tonight was the premiere episode of Butkus's new show, "Bound for Glory", and I was excited to see it. I settled in with some pizza, had the channel set and ready to go for 9:00. The program started with Dick Butkus driving into the small town in a big Ram Tough Dodge truck. He looked ominous as he chewed and puffed on a big old stogie. He set up the story of why he was there and the rest of the main characters were introduced. He was supposed to return a losing high school football program to their former winning ways. Unfortunately, the show quickly went off the rails after the opening sequences. It seemed to lack direction and it didn't feature enough of Butkus. By the end of it, I was disappointed. As big a football fan as I am, this was hard to watch. If Dick Butkus had not been in the show, I would have turned it off half way through. I was glad I didn't have to be a critic on this one.

I woke up early the next morning with the warm sun shining brilliantly through a crack in the window blinds. It was one of those Indian summer September days, and it was perfect! I did a little workout in my motel room, got some breakfast, and then formulated my day's plan. I set up the mini video camera on the passenger side of the rental car and filmed an intro for the journey.

McKee's Rocks was only about three hours away and I had all day to get there. I didn't actually have an appointment, but Mr. Butkus was aware that I would be showing up today or tomorrow. My plan was simple. I would arrive in the early afternoon, get the lay of the land, find McKee's high school, then show up during the after school football practice. This would give me an opportunity to see Dick Butkus from a distance and get myself used to his presence. God, I was nervous already and I hadn't even started traveling. "No problem," I thought. "The drive will calm me down. I'll enjoy it and the rest will take care of itself."

The countryside of upper New York and Pennsylvania were green with many gentle rolling hills. As the scenery passed, I would occasionally turn on the video camera, and talk about my feelings and hopes for the day. There were thoughts about my deceased Karate Sensei, Jimmy Mac, and how he would have loved to hear this story. I wished Erica and the kids were along for the adventure to help me capture the moment. The film would take their place, becoming a treasure for me, and my family for years to come.

I always looked forward to a road trip and today was no exception. I was getting close and I felt the excitement as my heart started to beat faster and stronger. Coming up to McKee's Rocks, I took exit #51, enjoying the synchronicity so much that I turned around and did it again, this time with the video camera rolling. My timing was perfect. I'd find the school, check into a motel and get settled in, allowing lots of time to get ready for the football practice and for Butkus.

McKee's Rocks was a pretty little town of about six thousand, with lots of American flags hoisted around the town. Driving down a winding, narrow road towards the school, I noticed "Spartan's Pride" signs on many front lawns. I loved it! You would never see this kind of community pride in Canada for anything, let alone a high school football team.

I went over a small hill, down into a valley. At the bottom, a yellow and black Spartan's Football banner was stretched high across the road. Somehow it made me feel proud. You have to admire the Americans for their community spirit! My first thought was how the banner reminded me of the opening scenes of the movie, "Brian's Song." My heart soared as I felt the emotion build in my belly, and I could hear the movie's bittersweet music in my mind.

Suddenly, with a left turn and jaunt up a short hill, I was at the school. At the entrance there was a barrier gate, complete with a security officer checking everyone's identification. "Good," I thought. "I have another opportunity to use my new business cards!"

"I'm here to see Dick Butkus," I stated while handing him my card.

He looked it over, saying, "Ya, Okay. Mr. Butkus just pulled in ahead of you. He's right over there in that blue dodge truck."

No! Not yet! I panicked and my blood pressure soared! Oh my God. I'm not ready. This isn't my plan. He can't be here now! I wanted to turn the car around and get the hell out of there as quickly as possible. The guard noticed my hesitation, motioned me forward, and then I was in. No turning back now. I parked the car, summoned up my courage, and flanked the large dodge truck, moving towards Dick Butkus. I took a couple of deep breaths and with a strong, confident voice I yelled, "Coach! Coach Butkus!"

The big man, with a head like a Brahma bull, turned slightly, cigar in hand, as his eyes focused on where the voice had come from. He was 6'3" with a classic brush cut - a football flattop. He wore a loose fitting t-shirt, khaki shorts, and was slightly hunched forward as if he were in a perpetual linebacker stance. He was in his early sixties, very trim, about 230 pounds. Apparently he shed about 15 lbs. from his "playing weight" after having open-heart bypass surgery a few years before. Still, he was a big man with a large frame.

"Coach Butkus. I'm Bob Mueller, Tough Guy Cards," I said as I extended my hand and offered him my business card. My small hand easily disappeared in this huge grip of the hand I had studied for years.

"Oh ya, the artist. Good to see you. Let's go to my trailer to talk," he said. Then he turned and started to lumber towards the office. Unprepared for the immediate meeting, I quickly excused myself and ran to the car to get my stuff. I grabbed my art portfolio with all the greeting cards and three original paintings. I looked at the video camera and remembered how I had passed up meeting Peyton Manning. "Screw it! I'm here. Just go for it," I told myself. "This may never happen again!" I grabbed the camera and ran to catch up with Butkus at his trailer/office. I was telling myself, "I'm doing okay. This is going to be fine. Just breathe and it will be okay. Just keep it simple, be professional, and try not to be an idiot fan!"

As we entered the office, I thought I should break the ice, so I said, "I saw your "Bound for Glory" show last night."

"Oh good. What did you think of it?" he asked earnestly.

"What did I think? Oh my god!" I panicked again. "Don't lie," I told myself. "Just tell the truth.

This was a stupid position I had put myself into, and as my mouth opened, I began to criticize my hero.

> **Bob's B.S.**
> If he thinks you are just a suck up fan he won't have any respect for you and the meeting will be over before it starts.

"Well … uh … I thought it started great and I really liked your entrance into the town. After that, I have to say I didn't really get it. It seemed to focus too much on the kids and players on the team. Not enough on you and frankly, I got a little lost," I said gently.

"The kids are the point, aren't they?" he remarked. "I talked to a few people today," Butkus retorted, "They liked it." I felt strike one. "Well anyways, let's see what you've got," he added.

After setting up the paintings around the office, I looked at the video camera then asked, "Do you mind if I set this up? I'd love to show it to my kids."

"Fine with me. Do what you like," he replied. His phone rang and he took the call, which was great for me as it gave me time to get my bearings and set up the camera. Everything seemed okay. If the camera bothered him, he didn't show, yet I had a sinking feeling. This was strike two and I hadn't even stepped up to the plate yet!

This is how I began the most excruciating 30 minutes of my life. I showed Dick the greeting cards and got a laugh or two out him as I nervously told him a bit of my story about becoming an artist. He asked a couple of questions and politely listened to me, but I couldn't shake the nerves or really get comfortable. I tried my best not to be an idiot fan, but I had no perspective other than the discomfort I felt and it would not go away. Simply put, I tried way too hard to make a good impression, constantly putting my foot in my mouth. I don't really know whether Dick noticed or cared, but the tension was palpable. I fumbled with everything and I created a deep angst I couldn't shake.

It's funny the things you think of when you are under stress. I wanted to absorb everything in those moments, yet my mind darted all over the place. Dick Butkus was in front of me, chewing and puffing on his cigar. He leaned back in his seat, as if to keep himself out of the video camera, only moving forward occasionally to look at a sample card. I noticed a long horseshoe-shaped scar on his right knee. That was the knee injury that shortened his career to just nine years. Moving down from the knee, I noticed he wore black NFL Reebok sneakers. I remembered the nickname he had as a Bears rookie. The veteran players named him "paddles" for his big 13 ½ double E wide feet. I wondered if he liked that name and whether he always wore NFL shoes. My mind kept wandering, "I wish I had bought a pair like that the last time I was in Chicago. Gee, his feet don't look that wide in the shoes. I wonder how strong those hands are?"

Perhaps I observed all these things and questioned them because I had read about them for so many years. Maybe the inner dialogue was an attempt to preoccupy my mind from the tension I felt. All I know for sure was, this wasn't the experience I had dreamed of. A number of calls came in for him as things started to get busy on the set. I remembered what Fred Richman had said about Dick Butkus with his work. It was about 30 minutes in and I figured that I had taken enough of his time as his day was just beginning. I had best take control and offer to leave, rather than to overstay my welcome.

As he finished his latest phone call I stood up and said, "Thank you for your time, coach. Just one last thing … If I could impose on you to autograph my paintings, I'd really appreciate it."

He looked at me, a little befuddled, saying, "I don't have a pen or anything here."

I quickly produced two Sharpie pens, one black and one silver. He sighed, actually he groaned, but dutifully and carefully signed the artwork. He didn't say a word, but I noticed the energy change and I felt the oxygen get sucked out of the room. He finished signing the last painting, then, keeping his back to me, he immediately left the trailer and was gone. I felt the anger in his mood, as well as the emptiness in the room and then as I packed up my stuff, in my soul. "Had I been too ballsy? Had I screwed up? Was it my fault?" I wondered. I don't really know what set him off, but definitely signing the paintings was over the top for him.

The film crew was there now and they set up for the day's shoot. I watched the football practice, the kids, and how everyone interacted. To add to my own sense of disappointment, I detected a lot of disrespect and apathy on the football side of this show. Didn't these kids understand the honor bestowed upon them? I was surprised at the lack of enthusiastic energy and the general laziness displayed by the players. From watching movies like "Friday Night Lights" and "Remember the Titans" I had the impression that high school football in the U.S.A. was a life and death experience. What I saw was a lackadaisical walk through with no emphasis on fundamentals or one-on-one drills.

Butkus took a group and did a little bag work with the

kids hitting the pads. It didn't look like anyone was really into it. In fact, it looked just the opposite. The players appeared to be more concerned with how they were looking, rather than how they were practicing. I remembered from my own football practices, how intense the coaches were - constantly yelling and pushing for more and more effort. I saw none of this and it was very disappointing to me.

I sat on the sidelines, sketching a little, and tried to make sense of what I was seeing as well as how I was feeling since my meeting. I didn't like what I saw, and I definitely didn't like how I felt. At the end of the practice, everyone, including the players, coaches and film crew left the field. They went to set up some additional shots and situations, so I left and headed for my motel room.

After getting some food, I thought about the day's events. I knew Erica was expecting me to call and share about the meeting. The sun was going down and, as I dialed, I dreaded telling her about my day. Erica answered the call on the second ring. There was joy in her voice, as she was so happy for me. I put the best spin on the event that I could, telling her about all the funny miscues of the day. Half way through my story, she stopped me in mid sentence. "It didn't go well, did it?" she questioned. "What happened?"

I told her how uncomfortable I'd felt and how I made a mess of it. Erica is always direct, but with a great deal of compassion. "Hon, I'm so sorry for you and I wish I could be there for you. You know, Fred Richman tried to tell you what to expect. You just didn't want to listen," she gently reminded.

"The truth …" I pondered. The truth is that I spent a sleepless night. I tossed and turned, thinking, what I might have done differently? In the morning I had come to the conclusion that I would go back to the site in the afternoon. I would thank Dick

Butkus again, give him the card portfolio for his future reference, and just let the chips fall where they may. After all, maybe I had misinterpreted things.

I went to the school site and waited for the big man to show. Right on time, he and a couple of the crew arrived to get ready for their day. Portfolio in hand, I quickly and confidently approached the group and, without hesitation, I went up to Dick and extended my hand. His eyes told me that he wasn't any happier today.

"Mr. Butkus, I'm on my way back to Canada, but I wanted to thank you again for your time and give you my portfolio," I said directly.

He shook my hand, without smiling he said grumpily, "Okay, but I don't have anywhere to put it."

"I understand," I insisted, "but I would really like you to have it."

He begrudgingly took it, walked over to his truck, and placed the portfolio on the front seat. "Okay, now we have a lot of work to do here," he grumbled dismissingly as he turned, then left to join the other crewmembers. There was no misinterpretation for me this time.

A few moments later, one of the crew ran over to me. "Hey, sorry about that. I don't know why that happens, but please don't take it personally. It's just kind of the way he is," he comforted.

My drive back to Toronto gave me six hours to reflect and think about what this event meant to me. It was time to apply some reason to this situation, rather than just feeling bad about it. I'd done enough soul searching the night before as to my own inadequate behavior. Erica was right. I knew in advance what might happen. I just didn't think it could happen to me! This left me to look at the truth. But what was the truth about what had happened here?

My mind went over it all again. Did I really do anything wrong? No. Did Butkus really do anything wrong? No. What was wrong was my diametrically opposed expectations of the meeting with Butkus.

Perhaps it was a problem of simple misunderstandings. This was just a casual meeting for Dick Butkus, but a once in a lifetime event for me. He didn't know what it meant to me and I didn't care how it imposed on him. Afterwards, it occurred to me that from the moment I met him, never once did I tell him that I admired him or why. I was so afraid of being some kind of suck up fan that I had actually created the opposite mood. I had criticized the work he was doing and I made every attempt to record the moment, rather than just enjoy it. I had shown him I wanted a piece of him instead of just saying how great a moment this was for me in my life, and sharing the joy of my work with him. I denied both of us the pleasure of the meeting.

It struck me, for the first time that I had never thought of Dick Butkus as a flesh and blood person. It was the image, the Chicago Bears, the orange, white and blue, and the number 51. The Dick Butkus I wanted to meet was the icon, not the man but he was a human being, flawed and imperfect, just like me. I wondered about what it was like to be him. What had it been like for him to be the biggest, baddest guy in his community since he had been a teenager? Imagine that, even in the world of professional football, where everyone is the best and everyone is big and tough, he had been the best of all time! He was the toughest man to ever play in the NFL! Wow! Imagine that...

"What kind of perspective would I have today if I had been the king of the mountain for my entire life? How would I have interacted with the world, if I had enjoyed his kind of power and success?" I wondered. Maybe the truth is that I wouldn't be as nice a person as he is. That was food for thought, and the thought nourished me.

> ### Bob's B.S.
> The mind is like a parachute; it only works when it is fully open. What opened for me was a deeper level of learning. The fact of the matter was this journey was mine and mine alone.

It had never been about Dick Butkus, as he was only the catalyst for my need to develop my talent.

The universe has a way of serving up a lesson when the student is ready to be taught. Although I had not felt ready, the meeting with Dick Butkus had shown me where my focus should be. The video camera had recorded me, with the lens focused on what I was doing, not him. He had intentionally kept himself out of the viewing screen. It was uncomfortable for me to watch, but it was real. It was presented to teach me another valuable lesson on my journey of self-discovery.

Remember to pay attention to the intention, particularly your intention. When you make yourself important enough for your needs to be met, you also have to be responsible for what happens. Sometimes "shit just happens!"

I had tried to deflect my true desires by making my journey about Dick Butkus. I had wanted to meet an icon, instead, I met a man. Now I had to decide what to do with this fact. Should I run away from it, letting it negatively dominate my thoughts and impressions? Maybe it could simply be a valley between the mountains, as part of the landscape of my Dick Butkus experiences. I had to choose between the truth of my direct experience and the iconic truth that had fueled my dreams for all these years.

"So you see, the fact is, it was Tom Donovan, not me, who shot Liberty Valance," said Jimmy Stewart to the reporter. "After 30 years I have finally told you the truth. Mr. Scott, now you tell me you won't use the truth as the story."

"No Sir," replied the reporter, "This is the west, sir, and when the legend becomes a fact, we shall print the legend!"

Bob's B.S.
Almost forty years before, I had made the legend of Dick Butkus my personal hero. I used his iconic image throughout my life as a source of inspiration.

The facts of who he was or who he might be didn't really matter.

"I'll keep the legend, too!" I thought.

Take-away

Be careful what you wish for!
Look for the learning in every situation
Pay attention to the intention.
What kind of success are you afraid of?
Is it business, personal, financial, or physical?
Who or what is on your chicken list to do?

Ubiquitous
u·biq·ui·tous [yoo-bik-wi-tuhs]
Adjective; existing or being everywhere, especially at the
same time; omnipresent: ubiquitous fog;
Ubiquitous little ants.

I first heard this word used during a show called:
"NFL Game of the Week." The broadcast highlighted the
Cleveland Browns giving the Chicago Bears their tenth loss
of what would be their worst season ever: 1 – 13.

The program, however, was less about the game than it was
about Middle Linebacker, Dick Butkus, who on that day
was, as Steve Sabol would write, ubiquitous.

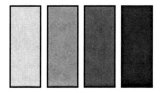

Desperate Times

Create Inspired Moments

The Forth Quarter

For a game to be epic, a classic remembered for years, a forth quarter comeback is mandatory. The lessons of the first three quarters bring you as far as skill and talent will allow. The forth quarter demands respect, as now you have three opponents: yourself, your rival and the clock.

"We didn't lose the game, we just ran out of time."   - Vince Lombardi

Now is crunch time. Do you want it? Yes or no? Can you rise to meet the challenge or will you fade away? If necessity is the mother of invention, ingenuity must surely be the father. My forth quarter began with a sense of forbidding defeat. I had outperformed and done better than anyone could have imagined. I took my talent to the limit and I had gone the distance, but I came up short. Perhaps time was telling me to let go of my dreams, accept reality, and acknowledge my loss … or not?

"Man's mind stretched to a new idea never goes back to its original dimensions." Oliver Wendell Holmes

I had found my Butkus ... then made a mess of it. Now I had to either find a way to make sense of my ordeal or let it go and move on. I had moved on many times before in my life, but this was different. I knew if I let this one go, the defeat would crush me. I looked for a reason that would excuse why I had failed so badly. Rather than blame or excuse myself, I needed to accept the experience in a way that supported me. Perhaps I had just wanted this experience so badly, I had not asked for it to be a good one. Perhaps I just wasn't ready. Perhaps it was a bit of everything, and now was not the time to ask why, but simply to ask how? What's next?

For the next six months I focused on painting other players and trying to diversify my concepts. I took advice from Bob Sgarlata and others to see if I could get "Tough Guy" Cards to become a quick success. Perhaps I could redeem myself in my own eyes, using the cards as my medium to succeed. As the months passed I became more restless and impatient. It seemed that every time something looked like it might go somewhere; it quickly became a dead end.

I began to notice I was less interested in painting and that the work was becoming a burden. The more I painted, the farther I got away from my goals. I thought I had done everything right. I had set high goals, created a time frame in which to accomplish them, and I had made huge strides towards fulfilling my dreams.

So why did I feel so lousy about what I had accomplished? The answer was simple. I wasn't having any fun because I wanted it to be more than it was, and it just wasn't. I was looking for an end result instead of enjoying the journey.

Bob's B.S.
Dis-satisfaction seeks change!

I put down my brush and canvas, and just let it be for a while. I was frustrated and I had lost my confidence. Rather than telling the universe what I wanted, I decided to listen. I waited and watched for a sign, a symbol ... something that would tell me what to do next.

"There will come a time when you believe everything is finished. That will be the beginning." Louis L'Amour

A few days later I awoke from an unusually deep and warm night's sleep. Feeling bright and optimistic, I started the day with my usual two cups of coffee. As I was checking my emails, I began thinking of my good fortune over the past year. I started to dream out loud again and it felt good. Today, for some reason, I let go of the expectation of moving forward and revisited the fun I had had.

Hell, I had actually met Dick Butkus ...nothing wrong in that! Are you kidding me? I had broken bread with the toughest National Football League S.O.B. ever, Dick – frigging - Butkus! Amazing! Simply amazing!

I was not going to feel bad about this anymore. I would remember what was real and most importantly, what I learned from it. I was renewed, and although my 30-minute rule for problems had taken a little longer this time, I was ready to move forward. I made a few calls to friends, including my son, Leigh, but no one was answering their phone that morning. "Well, maybe I'll write a letter," I thought, "but to whom?"

Who should I write?

A big grin came across my face and my eyes widened with excitement as an inspiring thought occurred to me. I'm going to write a letter to Steve Sabol! Yes, Steve Sabol, of NFL Films! I'll tell him about Dick Butkus and how I would love to see something new on TV about the old linebacker! He needs to hear my story.

Before writing a word, I said to Erica, "Guess who I'm writing? I'm writing Steve Sabol this morning. I'm going to tell him about my Dick Butkus adventure!" I don't remember what she said, but something to the effect of "That's nice.... who?"

I wrote with enthusiasm and passion, finding great joy. My dad had taught me years ago, if you have a complaint with a company, you should always write and address it to the President.

Bob's B.S.
Never write to an underling. Make sure you show that you mean business.

If it was good enough for complaints, surely writing the top man would work for compliments.

It was fun. It flowed, and it was exciting. I imagined if I told Steve Sabol about my 40-year journey, he would have to consider creating a new piece about Dick Butkus. It would be great to see more vintage Butkus tackles and his legendary intensity. I would also send him one of my own short karate films, particularly where I re-worked a montage of Dick Butkus, cutting it together with a Karate demonstration! I was so proud of my creation that I had already posted it on YouTube! Maybe Sabol would like it too.

Yes, this was fun, and through what I imagined would be a maze of employees; it might actually reach Steve Sabol. Hell, if I told NFL Films about my passion, maybe they would invite me to say something on camera. I could be the frothing fan, waving my Bears flag, Canada's Biggest Chicago Bears fan! Wouldn't that be something?

The next day, as I was getting the package ready to send to Mr. Sabol, the phone rang with a return call from my son. I immediately told him what I was doing and expected him to burst with his usual enthusiasm for my crazy ideas. Instead, the other end of the phone went oddly quiet.

Leigh said, "Dad, you know I always support you with your dreams about football, but I think this is a mistake. You know there are copyright laws about that Dick Butkus footage. You're going to get in trouble."

Surprised, I thanked him for his input and took his advice to heart. Perhaps I was being rash and had not thought this through. He was right. What if I got in trouble and ended up making a mess, creating problems for the Karate Schools? I took my package and placed it at the bottom of a pile of papers on my desk.

I forgot about the package for the next few days. Then, by chance, I was reviewing a DVD called, "The Secret." This was a new product in the market that retold the story of the old universal law known as the "Law of Attraction." I had been a student of such teachings for decades, so I was interested in this new presentation. It was somewhat underwhelming, with lots of glitz and not a lot of meat. However, as I have taught my own students, if you go to a seminar and get just one idea, then you have received full value. This was no exception.

A gem appeared when the gentleman on the screen stated, "If you have a good idea, do not hesitate. Do it immediately!" I rewound the disc to "do it immediately," playing it again and again! Yes, that was it! I immediately picked up my package, filled it with positive thoughts, even kissed it, and mailed it off to NFL Films. I let it go with a deep sense of fulfillment.

A few weeks later, I received a phone call from a New Jersey number. "This is Keith Cossrow calling from NFL Films," said an official sounding, lawyer-like voice. "Is this Bob Mueller?" he asked.

I answered affirmatively and, before he could say anything else, I asked, "I have a question before you start … am I in trouble? Am I in trouble with the NFL?"

"Trouble? No. Why would you be in trouble with us?" Cossrow questioned openly. I explained my pirating of Dick Butkus footage, to which he laughed and said, "Well, perhaps if you had sent your letter to anyone other than Steve, you might be in trouble! We like your story and we want to do it. I'm calling to book a time with you in July. We'll send a film crew to your home!"

The next day a post card showed up with a Bruno Nagurski stamp on it from NFL Films. The plain white, card stock paper had the NFL Films logo and a hand-written note:

BOB –
THANKS FOR THE DVD AND YOUR KIND WORDS ABOUT NFL FILMS!
IF WE HAVE ANOTHER TV SPECIAL ON DICK BUTKUS, AND ONE IS IN THE PLANNING STAGES RIGHT NOW, WE WILL DEFINITELY INCLUDE YOUR WORK AND YOUR STORY.
BEST STEVE

Wow! The President of NFL Films took the time to write a card to me! A film crew is coming to Kelowna to interview me about Dick Butkus. I am speechless! Who would have thought that a man that important would read his own mail? This was the first of many surprising things that I would learn about Mr. Steve Sabol and NFL Films.

After the first day's shooting, the NFL Films guys returned to their hotel to decompress and plan for the next day. The crew consisted of director/producer, Keith Cossrow, cinematographers, Steve Andrich and Frankie Lasar, along with a sound tech and a local lighting roadie. At first blush they seemed like an ordinary bunch of guys. I found out, over the next few days, that they were actually highly touted and acclaimed filmmakers. They arrived early in the morning and immediately began transforming our home into various 'locations' to get the day's shoot. Keith took me aside, explaining his basic plan and his ideas about capturing the story he had been sent to film. One of those ideas was to set up lighting in my small art room and film me painting.

"You want to film me painting?" I asked with a little disbelief. "How long are you thinking?"

"We will be set up within the next half hour, say by 9:30, so we should be able to get it in by noon or so," he said, rather matter-of-factly. "You just paint like you usually do and I'll ask you a few questions. I think this will be the back bone of the piece," he declared.

Oh my god! Talk about a boring plan! It will be like watching grass grow or literally watching paint dry. I had laid out a bunch of ideas for filming karate and yoga. I also invited guests like my old football coach, Roy Vollinger, and as much family as could make it. This guy, Keith, wants to watch me paint? I thought this was going to be about Dick Butkus, action and intensity! "Okay Keith. Whatever you want me to do. I'm ready," I said, and we started to work.

Cossrow was a very friendly, but direct person and this obviously wasn't his first rodeo. Whatever this was going to be, it was in his hands. I had organized three canvases to help show the process I take when painting. I was a little nervous at first, as we had five grown men, lights and cameras all in my 11 x 13 upstairs art room. With cameras on either side of me, and even one shooting in slow motion, we began. I remember thinking, "A two camera shoot and slow-mo just to film a guy paint. These guys are way over the top! No wonder NFL Films is the best in the business! I wonder what this is costing just to get a few lines about my Dick Butkus story."

As I started to paint I began to feel comfortable and it was nice to talk to Keith. He said that he would do a more formal interview later on, but for now we'd just talk so they could get the shots they wanted. He would scope out some of the story and piece it together as the day went on. We talked and laughed, and I painted. It was actually great fun!

About an hour into it I caught Keith glancing over to Frankie Lasar quietly mouthing some words like, "This is great!" That struck me as being odd, since all we were doing was talking as I painted, but I could feel their positive energy. They were definitely excited about what they were getting on film. We did a more formal interview later and a few other things, but it was the painting and the talking that had created a buzz.

At the end of the afternoon, they packed up and went back to their rooms at "The Cove" Waterfront Hotel. We would finish the day's shoot there, where I had an art show set up, and then do the following day's filming at the same location.

Erica and I, along with a couple of our brood, had also booked rooms at "The Cove" for that evening. We had our dinner and then decided to go to the bar for a glass of wine. Beside us, in the adjacent dining room, the "NFL Films" guys were eating and digesting the day's events.

My son in-law, Leith, who is always thoughtful and somewhat mischievous, decided it would be good fun to send the boys a round of drinks to wash down their meal. Keith came over and thanked us but said they really couldn't, as it had been a long day and the next morning would come early.

They did however take delivery of the libations, and then got ready to leave. As they were settling their check, a round of shooters showed up and Leith was grinning. Although they protested, the crew dutifully complied. Then came another round and another after that. Leith had instructed the waiter to keep them coming every 10 minutes until the staff heard otherwise from him.

Cossrow, as the leader, had to make a decision. He had given up trying to refuse, so he sent a retaliatory volley of shooters back at us! A truce then ensued, as we joined company at their table and made it a magnificent evening of trading 'war' stories. As one of my oldest friends, a Scotsman complete with the Scottish brogue and the swagger, likes to say, "Don't tell me what you think, Laddie - tell me your heart." It was that kind of night. We shared many insights - or at least they seemed insightful, given the barrage of refreshments!

I was amazed to find out what an accomplished crew these guys were. They all marveled at Steve Andrich's filming talent and his live action shooting ability, saying he was the best in the business. Keith said that he had won an Emmy Award for a story about a rogue bar in Philly and, based on our day's shooting, he had a very good feeling about my Butkus story. I grilled them on who they had filmed and met what they were like, who was the coolest they had ever met, and all that kind of stuff. "Have you ever met Joe Namath? Next to Butkus, he's one of my favorites!" I shared.

"Joe ... Yes, what a man!" and they all smiled. "He always shows up with a blonde," quipped Frankie Lazar. "Hey! He's Joe Willie frigging Namath!"

Can you imagine what a little piece of heaven this was

for me? These guys were so down to earth, seemed to know everything about everything, and they were talking to me! It was hog heaven for sure! "What's it like to work at NFL Films?" I asked.

"Are you kidding? Hell, we watch football for a living and get paid to do it!" they all smiled in agreement. Yes, hog heaven. I asked Keith specifically about his process, and how things worked at NFL Films.

"What was Steve Sabol really like?" I asked ten times, in ten different ways. Frankly, I don't remember much about the answers. I do remember, vividly, the feeling of warmth and the admiration they all had for Steve and the entire organization.

"You know the big painting you did of Butkus on the bench?" Keith asked.

"Yes. That is my favorite." I responded.

"Did you know that image is the most famous shot in the entire history of NFL Films?" he continued. "Do you know who got that shot? ... Steve Sabol!" He went on to explain how the guys on the sidelines were called moles and on that particular day in Chicago, Steve had been the one to crawl through the mud to get the "bloody hands shot."

"Yah, Steve has a knack for that. He sees the drama. Did you know he's also an artist?" Keith boasted. "You know, the big music, the voice of god, the big finale!" We all laughed, then spontaneously, everyone joined in a short musical rendition "bum ta da bum, ta da a bum, bum, bum ...bum" (I could see old Raider Willie running in slow motion.) "He is not just a film artist you know, but an artist like you. He personally decorated the entire NFL Films building with pictures and memorabilia. He also has some of his own art work hanging there." Keith finished. Steve was the consummate artist and NFL Films made art first and money second. The iconic Bob

Dylan once said, "What's money? A man is a success if he gets up in the morning and goes to bed at night and in between does what he wants to do."

I was surprised about the artist connection. I don't really know why, but it did put some questions in my mind. It occurred to me, perhaps my original fascination with Butkus, might not have its origins as I had always thought. Past that, I was curious about how things happen to create a piece for the "NFL Films Presents" show.

Keith explained how the writing was the key factor, and about all the stages it takes to get ready for the broadcast. I found it fascinating and I could have listened all night. He told of the entire facility, particularly the screening theater, how the theater is used to debut all the finished pieces in front of the entire creative staff, including Steve.

The point is to "defend the piece" as it was being scrutinized by your colleagues. He downplayed the critical part of the sessions, saying the key point was to explain why you used a scene or didn't, getting feedback on what might be improved upon. As an amateur moviemaker (who isn't these days?) I was very impressed. I got a whole new understanding of how much care and thought goes into every piece that winds up on a TV. Then, thinking about Keith's Emmy Award comment, I questioned, "So, what makes for a successful piece and how do you know when it's good?"

He didn't say it right then but he knew there had been some kind of magic in the art room that day. He had used a classic technique to make me comfortable, and once he had my mind open, he found what he had come for. Looking back now, I see that he got into my unconscious thoughts, my dreams, by having me paint. It is like when you are driving a car and don't remember anything about the trip. You are on "autopilot," lost in your own thoughts. Yes, Cossrow was a master at getting his subjects to open up and give him that extra something which others might have missed.

By now, everyone was well into their drinks and all the Films guys were part of the conversation. After hearing my question about what makes for a good piece, they all kind of looked at each other and said almost in unison, "When Steve likes it."

Keith paused and after a thoughtful moment he said, "I think the bottom line is, we all want to please Steve. It's that simple. If he gets it, we know we have something worthwhile."

The next morning everyone was fresh faced and on the job for the 8:00 a.m. call time. Despite the late night festivities we did a long and full day of "action shooting." I taught the various components of karate and yoga that would make up the remainder of the film which I began to realize, was more about me than it was about Dick Butkus.

Over the next few months I kept in contact with Keith, as he needed extra photographs and additional background information. When the new football season returned in the fall, I had something new to look forward to. "NFL Films Presents" was going to feature me on national TV! It couldn't happen soon enough as far as I was concerned!

In the mean time, I felt so grateful for my experience that I wanted to make a gesture of thanks. I sent Steve Sabol the #1/51 limited edition print of my favorite painting. Now that I knew this was Steve's baby long before it was mine, the gift seemed appropriate. "Butkus on the Bench" said it all, whether as a piece of art on a canvas or on a film. It showed the power and the pathos of the man, framed in a Rembrandt like setting of darkness and light. It was motionless, almost timeless, while alive with active thought. It was the image that had fueled the fires of my teenage obsession with Dick Butkus and with art. I was grateful to have the opportunity to give a gift to a great man, and that doesn't happen very often.

I started checking out the Canadian TSN Sports channel to see when they were broadcasting new "NFL Films Presents" shows. I was shocked to discover they had a 2 -3 week delay from the original broadcast dates shown on ESPN in the USA. This would mean that I could not see the original show until almost a month after its release date and for me, this was unacceptable.

I devised a plan to drive about 100 miles to the USA border and get a motel room in Omak, WA. I could then see the show in Washington State on the original broadcast date. Now all I had to do was wait for the call from Keith. September and October passed, and as we got into November there was still no word from NFL Films.

Finally, during the third week of November, just before the American Thanksgiving celebration, Keith called. The episode was called "Midwest Legends" and it featured a piece about the old Minnesota Vikings HOF coach, Bud Grant, and me. I was thrilled to find out that they were using my title, ""Finding Your Butkus"," for the segment. As a synchronistic footnote Bud Grant had been hired as the coach of the Winnipeg Blue Bombers in January 1956, the year of my birth in Winnipeg Manitoba.

The confirmed broadcast was now set for Monday, November 26th, the day after my 51st birthday! This was when I truly started to notice the synchronicity of the events that were happening to me.

I watched the premier of ""Finding Your Butkus"" at 9:30 a.m. on a Monday morning. I was in a dingy, cold concrete block motel room in the small border town next to Osoyoos, B.C. Although the setting left something to be desired, it was a triumph and I hung on every word. I was amazed then, as I am to this day, that Keith was able to tell my story so effectively and succinctly in such a short amount of time. The whole segment of ""Finding Your Butkus"" amounted to 11 ½ minutes in total.

Later, when discussing my newfound fame, I would tell people that Andy Warhol had got it wrong. In his famous statement he said, "In the future, everybody will be world famous for fifteen minutes."

> ### Bob's B.S.
> What he didn't know was that your fifteen minutes comes with commercial time. It's actually only 11 ½ minutes!!

Keith had captured the humor and the madness in my story. He had also found the heart of my unexpected journey into the synchronicity of "self." His skill as a storyteller was impressive. Steve Sabol was a good teacher.

When I sent Keith a "Tough Guy" thank you card, he told me my story would be part of the NFL Films submissions for Emmy consideration in the coming year. He also said Steve Sabol had enjoyed the story and had placed my painting of Dick Butkus at the doorway to the Ed Sabol Theater. It was a special honor that marked both Steve's appreciation for my painting and the significance of the shot that he had taken forty years before. This was incredible. Now I was officially a part of the history of NFL Films. Just the thought of my art hanging at the Mecca of football creativity gives me chills to this day.

The next thrill came again as a phone call. "Bob, it's Keith, I just got the confirmation that "Finding Your Butkus" has been nominated for an Emmy Award in the Outstanding Long Feature category. But before you get all excited, I have to tell you that we don't have a chance in hell of winning!" He went on to explain that we were one of five nominees and although we were good, the others in this group were very strong.

"Our competition is like this," he explained, "Do you remember last year that Coach Bill Walsh died? Well, there is a great piece about him, as well a show about the soccer team that crashed in the Andes and engaged in cannibalism to survive, a treasured horse who also died, and then some other death and destruction story ... and what do we have? We got a guy who is having a great life and likes to paint!" Keith laughed and I joined with him.

"You're right, we have no shot," and we laughed again. Keith told me that when it comes to awards, the Emmys love tragedies. The chances of us winning in this category were at least 50 – 1 odds against, maybe more.

"I wouldn't recommend you coming all this way to New York. It just isn't worth it! Hell, I won't even be at the Emmys this year. I'm filming a feature length film in Europe about the Lemans Auto Race," he said.

I thanked him for his forthright honesty but let him know that no matter what, we would be there! I had never been to New York City, or to an Award Ceremony like the Emmys. Erica hadn't either, and we would definitely be present for this. I couldn't think of any reason that could make me not want to go. A weekend in NY and the chance to be at an elite event as part of NFL Films ...are you kidding me? Winning, losing, who cares? Either way, this was the biggest win ever for me, and I wasn't going to miss it.

Every part of New York was magic, even the initial arrival. The city is just one big icon after another. On the approach, overlooking the city, you can see all the famous buildings. The ones you have seen hundreds of times in photos, movies, and on TV. Unlike other cities, where there might be one or two landmarks such as the Eiffel Tower or the Golden Gate Bridge, there are literally dozens of renowned monuments visible from the air. Strangely, it was like "going home," particularly seeing the Statue of Liberty. That "lady" was the gateway to the United States of America, and I found the sight of her as both odd and inspiring.

The biggest surprise for me was the people of the Big Apple. For many years I had heard about the legendary attitude and abruptness of the typical New Yorker. After all, this was Gotham City. We had better be on our toes, or we would get stepped on. It was just the opposite, as the people we met were attentive, helpful, and so cosmopolitan. With everyone living so close together, we quickly realized that in order to survive in New York you needed to be considerate, or at the very least be tolerant of other people's backgrounds. It seemed that every ethnic variety from across the world was represented on every block. New Yorkers had their unique accent and particular style of speaking. Their conversations were often fast-paced and seemed a bit aggressive, but they also took the time to be of service. The Big Apple, for all its hustle and bustle, was friendlier than most small towns I have visited. There were no suspicious looks from some small-minded locals, just a matter of fact attitude of "you're here, so get on with it and fit in." I was impressed with that.

After a few days of sight seeing, it was finally Monday, April 28th, show time! The 29th Annual Sports Emmy Awards were held at Frederick P. Rose Hall, Lincoln Center, located in The Time Warner building at the foot of Columbus Circle. It's a large, modern building that backs onto the west side of Central Park. Going up the long glass escalators, we took in the city views, as we approached the top floor and the entrance for the momentous event. Continuing through the lobby and into a large room for the pre–event cocktail party we found hundreds of sports writers, TV personalities, producers and executives milling around in front of a 20 foot high glass wall that overlooked Central Park. What a magnificent view!

I looked around to see if I recognized anyone. I immediately spotted Charles Barkley, the basketball legend turned announcer, along with a few other "talking heads" from various broadcasting stations. I hoped I might see the old Raiders Coach, John Madden, but apparently he didn't show up this year to receive his perennial Emmy as the top sports caster in the business. He had about fifteen of them!

As I was scanning the room, I felt a tap on my shoulder and turned to see a friendly, smiling face. Chris Barlow introduced himself and his associate, Vince. "Bob Mueller? I'm Chris Barlow with NFL Films. I work with Keith. It's a pleasure to meet you! There are a bunch of us at the back of the room. Come and I'll introduce you and Erica." That was the start to a magical evening with some great people. For the next hour, Chris told us what to expect from the evening and shared some stories about Keith.

As part of the conversation, I shared Keith's prediction regarding our "50 – 1" chance of winning an Emmy for ""Finding Your Butkus"." Everyone laughed and chimed in, one way or another saying, "At least! It's probably more like

80 to 100 -1, but we're glad to meet you and it's great that you came all this way!" During the conversation, the NFL Films people were talking about how they had been shut out last year, with no wins. There was also mention of the recent staff lay offs for the first time ever. The new NFL Network had been a bigger money drain than expected, and there was a lot of pressure being put on by the NFL owners to cut costs.

This was nothing new. Even back to the days when Ed Sabol had started the company, the owners of the teams wanted steak for the price of hamburger. The Sabols had proven for decades that quality was actually cost efficient, as a great story and a great product could be shown over and over. NFL Films were the image-makers and no one argued with the fact that their work had helped make the game what it is today. I enjoyed hearing the insider information and was reminded that this was a business first, no matter how I, as a fan, may feel about it.

The curtain call came and we all wished each other "luck." Chris and the Films team went down to the main floor and we headed to our private seats on the right side of the balcony. I looked at the program to see when ""Finding Your Butkus"" was scheduled for nomination. The category was near the end, along with the "Broadcaster of the Year" (which was similar to the best man at the Oscars.) Being a movie buff, I immediately got the idea that the "Outstanding Long Feature" was equivalent to the "Best Picture Award" at the Oscars! That sounded great to me and I figured it would be a nice qualifying statement for the future. I guess I was already working on my acceptance speech …accepting the expected loss, that is!

As the evening went on, I could feel the tension in my body, and the vibrational buzz of the competition. I wondered, with great anticipation, "How will it feel to hear the announcement? What clip of the feature will they show? Will I be in it?" I loved the excitement and, although I believed the predictions about losing, I kept thinking, "What if?" I thought about Keith Cossrow and wished that he were here. I really liked him, his energy, and his self-effacing humor. His presence would have added so much more to the experience.

Then the moment was upon us. The presenters, Chris Collingsworth and Joe Buck, began listing and showing the film clips on the stage screen. As I heard ""Finding Your Butkus"" mentioned, I saw myself on the big screen. I also began a chanting in my head, saying to myself, "FYB – FYB - FYB - FYB." I squeezed Erica's arm, digging my fingers in as they announced, "And the winner is… "FINDING YOUR BUTKUS" - NFL Films, Steve Sabol, Chris Barlow, Keith Cossrow - producers. With the applause, Chris made his way to the stage for the second time that evening.

I felt the need to be part of it.

I put my hands to the side of my mouth and yelled as loud as I could, "Atta boy, Keith!" My gesture wasn't lost on Chris, who immediately put his arm up to acknowledge my cheer for the creative man who couldn't be there. I felt my face burning with joy. It was unbelievable! We had won! 50 -1 be damned – what a feeling! What a moment! It had been too much to hope for!

Barlow, a very polite man, thanked the people who needed to be thanked, and then looked up at the balcony saying, "We have Bob & Erica Mueller in the audience this evening. They traveled all the way from British Columbia, Canada to be here tonight." The audience was generous with their acknowledgement and applause. Chris had returned my gesture for Keith and paid it forward. Once again, NFL Films showed themselves to be a classy outfit.

What seemed like moments later, we were back in the

lobby. Chris appeared with the team, holding two golden Emmy Awards. The statues were beautiful and we were thrilled when he invited us to hold one and have some pictures taken. As part of the buzz in the room we overheard a few people saying things like, "Can you believe the Butkus piece won? ... should have been Bill Walsh." etc, etc! I guess everyone was surprised! For me it was like the 69 Jets / Colts again and God, how I loved to be the underdog! I never got tired of it. Be it "Rudy," or "Brian's Song," or ""Finding Your Butkus"," it felt great to beat the odds and win!

We all proceeded to the floor below and met in the bar to celebrate. It was great fun! Everyone was high with excitement. NFL Films had won a total of five Emmys that night and there was a sense of pride, as well as a sense of relief.

I told my Butkus stories and listened intently about the workings at NFL Films. There was a lot of talk about how the wins tonight would assist in saving jobs and help keep some of the great programming intact. It really felt good knowing that my story was now part of NFL Films history (the 95th Emmy to be exact) and that it had participated in helping the company! After many celebratory glasses of red wine, we retired to our hotel room and rest. Tomorrow would be our last day in New York.

The morning came early and we rushed out of the hotel to get a rental car for the drive to Mt. Laurel, New Jersey. Our car was ready for 8:00 a.m. and we were quickly on the road. Unfortunately, we were driving in the wrong direction, away from the "tunnel" which led out of the city to the Jersey turnpike. Of all the things people have commented on, by far the most common is, "You drove a rental car in New York City? Are you crazy? What was it like?" I'll tell you what was it like? It was ... SLOW! You quickly learned that every road was like a maze and if you saw an opening or a hole in the traffic, you stuck the nose of the car into it. Failure to do so would result in immediate reactions from the people behind you. Nobody minded if you butted in. It was expected. As long as we were inching forward, everyone was happy.

Our last New York day would be in New Jersey, close to Philadelphia PA. I find it amazing just how close together all the large cities are in. New York, Philadelphia, Boston, etc. are only a few hours drive by car! Philly was only about 90 miles away, so once we got on the freeway, the travel went fast!

Soon we were in Mt. Laurel, New Jersey and looking for the NFL Films Building. I don't know how big this city is, but it looked very clean and well kept. I would guess that NFL Films was one of the biggest employers in the area, with about 300 employees. After a few miscues we found our destination - One NFL Plaza, the site of a very large and modern three-story building.

The sign said "NFL FILMS!" It gave me tingles and still does. As we entered the building, we saw rows upon rows of EMMY Awards in the lobby. For the next hour or so Chris Barlow was our host. He guided us through all three levels, some 300,000 sq. ft. in all. The building had a large rectangle layout and long hallways with producer's offices on the outside perimeters. On the inside were large rooms of technical studios for mixing and recording the finished work. We saw the sister-sets for the NFL Network, Steve's "NFL Films Presents" locations, a large orchestra room for producing all the legendary sound tracks, and the most amazing sound mixing suite I had ever seen.

The highlight for me was in the hallways. I really hadn't understood what Keith had meant about Steve Sabol decorating the building. Seeing is believing. And what I saw was the most impressive collection of football items and memorabilia possible. Large photos of famous moments in football history, pieces of art with many famous painters represented, and lots of old 1940's type posters and pin ups.

I also noticed John Wayne and Burt Lancaster movie posters and wondered if Steve was also a big fan of these characters. "Who am I kidding? If they were on his walls, he probably knew all this movie stuff inside out!" Then at one point, I thought I had caught an intimate glimpse of Steve Sabol.

It was near a section that Chris said was a favorite shoot location for Steve's interviews. The spot had a couple of leather chairs, with extensive shelving full of helmets, toys and antique football games. I knew I had seen those backgrounds before.

Now it was close to noon, and Chris mentioned we would grab some lunch with a couple of the guys. I just wanted to go back and stare at the hallways and all the historic memories. I could have spent hours, maybe days, just looking at everything.

Off to lunch, we unexpectedly doubled back to where Steve's own artwork was hanging and spent a few minutes looking at his pieces. They were unique, so different from anything else we had seen. There were all kinds of symbolic items, mixed with photos and images that went back many decades. The frames were intricate and actually part of the art in many of the pieces. I wished that I could get an explanation of what they meant. The more I looked at them, the more they piqued my curiosity and filled my head with questions.

This area was also the shooting location where I thought I had seen Steve. Chris excused himself for a moment and asked us to have a seat. There was a little commotion as a number of staff members gathered around. When he returned, we followed him past the toy displays, into a corner office.

Looking into the large office there were about ten people, including cinematographer, Frankie Lasar. He and the others were hovering around a big desk. There was another camera at the other side of the room. Lasar, along with his camera, had a big, pie-eating grin on his face and, as our eyes met, he winked and raised his eyebrows in a "knowing" way. "A two-camera shoot ... of what?"

As I wondered, I noticed a man with a very distinctive full head of hair, bending over the desk and shuffling some papers around. It was Steve Sabol!

He looked up, said something to the person next to him, and came around the desk holding a golden idol. His voice was silky and full, exactly as I had heard for decades. I wish I could tell you what he said, but my mind was busy grasping to understand what my eyes were seeing. I instantly knew what I was looking at, but I can't say that I believed it.

"I'd like to present this Emmy to you, Bob," Steve declared. ""Finding Your Butkus" is a story that will be played for years to come. It's the kind of story that we like to tell here at NFL Films."

That statement is forever etched in my brain.

This poignant moment was unexpected and I was completely overwhelmed. Gratefully, I accepted this personal Emmy from "the voice, the man and perhaps the myth of a man" I was just starting to know. The assembled producers applauded and smiled. They, as long time members of NFL Films, were used to this kind of wonderful gesture by Steve Sabol.

For my part, I tried to give something back in the form of a thank you, saying to Steve that he probably didn't know how important NFL Films was to millions of us fans ... I'm pretty sure he does know! I was full of emotion, not particularly wanting to blubber in front of the crew, but really not caring if

I did. So, in typical fashion, I did neither, but everyone knew that this was incredibly special for me.

I had learned years ago, on stage at the Royal Theater in Victoria B.C., that life consists of just a few extraordinary moments. Like the saying, "There is no second chance to make a good first impression," I have learned the power of creating special moments for others. It is the sweetest gift you can give another. The impact of witnessing a birth, tying a well-deserved Black Belt on a karate student, or a few words in the right moment can create a memory that lasts a lifetime. Almost twenty years ago, I had created a lasting Zen-like moment as I awarded a special student the rank of "Sensei." The power of that moment taught me the true sweetness of life. It created a memory in my mind that, to this day, I still feel, hear, and taste.

On this day, in his office, Mr. Steve Sabol had done that for me. The Emmy Award was the memento to take home, but the moment was the true gift.

Take-away

Listen to the idea that whispers in your ear
rather than the voice that occupies your head.
Recall a moment in your life where
you were overcome with happiness.
Were you the giver or the receiver of this gift/moment?
Can you see it, hear and taste it? Can you feel it?
What events do you associate with your greatest joy?
Are they rewards you received or sacrifices you made?

Synchronicity and Steve Sabol

The Post Game Synopsis

After playing my four quarters and getting a huge win, it was time to reflect and look for the meaning. For me the realization came as déjà vu experience. Why had "Finding Your Butkus" found such appeal? What had Sabol seen that caused him to take a chance on this story? Why had this been so important to me?

"How old would you be if you didn't know how old you are?" - Satchel Paige.

Fifteen. I had been fifteen for the past four years. From the moment I remembered the Butkus image of my youth, and picked up the paintbrush, I had dreamed like a child. Like an awestruck teenager, every part of the adventure had made juvenile sense. Nothing was practical and everything was play, therefore everything was possible.

The post mortem answers provided a simple synchronistic truth: I had done this before. Déjà vu! Forty years before I was a fascinated teenager receiving accolades from my football art. When I returned to my art, I knew the path to joy and found my voice. When I ran to the mountaintop and yelled to be heard, I noticed a forty-year old echo that had been waiting for me.

"Tell me a fact and I'll learn, tell me a truth and I'll believe.

But tell me a story, and it will live in my heart forever." - Steve Sabol

The heart of this story lives here:

It was another dark Sunday for the NFL's oldest franchise, the Chicago Bears. This was the bleakest season they had ever experienced. The clouds that covered Wrigley Field that day delivered more rain than snow, as the windy city dispensed its gusts of discontent. With just two games left in the 1969 season, the mighty Bears had amassed just one win against eleven losses.

Today's effort, a classic Packers vs. Bears tilt, would not shed any new light on their season. By the middle of the fourth quarter they were losing again, down 21-3. One field goal for the offence, and no magic left in the legs of Gale Sayers, had created lots of playing time for the defense.

That was just fine for the Chicago fans.

They may lose the wars, but when the ubiquitous Dick Butkus was on the field, they never lost a battle.

Long before there was a steel curtain in Pittsburgh, there were the Monsters of the Midway in Chicago. As the most feared man in football, middle linebacker, Dick Butkus, did not take kindly to losing. There was nothing "cloak and dagger" about how he and the Bears were going to defend their pride on this or any other day.

They would create a no-man's land of mud and blood, and crush any player who dared to run between the tackles. Butkus made sure of that. His bigger-than-life play made his intimidating style of growling, spitting and cursing almost as entertaining as his huge hits and tackles.

Butkus played in the middle for all to see and he didn't hide from anyone.

Another man, behind the curtains like the Wizard of Oz, was on the sidelines. He too was all knowing and, like Butkus, was seemingly everywhere at once. Steve Sabol was not, however, from Oz. This wizard worked behind the lens of a camera during the early days of NFL Films. His world had him join the players in the trenches, down where the action was. When the Sabols were on the gridiron, they created art where once there had only been sport. Before the masterful work of Ed and Steve Sabol, there had only been winners and losers with team standings, and scoring plays. Now there were heroes, villains, and stories, lots and lots of stories.

The opposing quarterback today was future Hall of Famer, Bart Starr. His Green Bay Packers had been held to just two scores, but near the game's end he was driving towards a third. On the scoreboard, the Bears offense was badly outplayed. But this was not the case for the Bears defense. Series after series, Starr's time clock domination created bad field position for the Bears, but time after time Butkus' defense remained stout. They may have been out-gunned, but they weren't out-manned!

But, this last Packer's touchdown was a back breaker, and now the game was lost. Defeat was as certain today, as the rain and the mud.

On the Bear's bench, the defensive platoon aligned much like they did on the field, sitting man to man and almost in formation. They hunched forward, shielding themselves from both the elements and the disappointment. The defense left their helmets on as the rain spat down and the mud caked in between their cleats. The big man in the middle, sitting between his defensive ends, Dick Evey and Ed O'Bradovich stared vacantly into the face of the loss that was just moments away.

Dick Butkus, his knuckles bloody and taped, had his huge hands clasped together as he absorbed the final, frustrating minutes in the mud, the blood and the rain. There it was a spectacle of motionless action, and a moment of truth that no artist could resist.

When the wizard saw it, he crawled on his hands and knees to make it his own. The few seconds of film captured the moment. The story it told, created an enduring image that inspired many careers, particularly mine.

"Synchronicity is the experience of two or more events as meaningfully related, where they are unlikely to be causally related. The subject sees it as a meaningful coincidence." – Webster's Dictionary

My own irresistible beginning of noticing synchronistic events would not happen for another 40 years. Before I could discover my true adult desires, I would need to revisit my boyhood passions, find my inner artist, and relive a long lost memory of a childhood confrontation.

For me, as an eight-year old boy in Winnipeg, Manitoba, my alignment with football began at about the same time the Sabols created NFL Films. Although I had never actually seen a football game at that time, I passed on other forms of balls, birds and pucks to play and throw a football.

"What do you know about playing football?" the large and slightly over weight boy demanded. A bunch of young boys were playing at the schoolyard in the "married quarters" section of the CFB Air Force base that I called home.

"I know lots about football!" I argued "And I'll be a quarterback some day!" As a third grader, I wanted to be heard.

"I draw pictures of players all the time and I'm great!" I declared.

Rory, a year older, was bigger and stronger than I. He was known for his big mouth and as a bully who liked to push his weight around. "Ya, well you're too small to be any good!" he yelled. "All you can do is draw football players! You can't play! Can you? Art boy!" he taunted.

A schoolyard skirmish is how I remember my introduction to wanting to prove my desires about football. I wanted to be a player, and be the kind of hero who could overcome his boyish doubts! Art was my way to express the passion I felt for the game I loved from the very first time I saw it.

When my art turned into martial arts, I learned about developing myself as a physical art. Part of learning martial arts is developing a strong mind and creating an effective ability to focus. This combination of both mental and physical concentration aligns with your inner thoughts, desires, and ultimately the true nature of your "self." Synchronizing your "self" with your desires naturally attracts like-minded ideas and people.

The law of attraction, as outlined in Charles F. Haanel's book from 1912, "The Master Key," states that "Like Attracts Like." Napoleon Hill later wrote in "Think and Grow Rich," that whatever the mind can conceive and believe, it can achieve. These teachings are likely responsible for my ability to recognize how my 40-year odyssey came to be.

"Synchronicity is the experience where the subject connects dissimilar events as having a meaningful coincidence."

"Like Attracts like," flashed in my mind, as I said "What you are looking for is looking for you!" Emmy Award in hand,

I began my speech at the greatest art show of my life. The audience had just seen the NFL Film's segment about me and now I was telling the audience the story behind ""Finding Your Butkus"."

This was the Steve Sabol /Bob Mueller Art Show – and for me a dream come true. Held in Canton Ohio, home of the NFL Hall of Fame, my "Tough Guy" paintings hung in a gallery along with Steve Sabol's legendary art. During the past year, I had worked at a manic pace to paint and produce a collection of artwork that I called the "NFL Films Top 10 Players of All Time." This opportunity had come along, as did all of my adventures, when I asked the right question, to the right person, at the right time.

Months earlier, Steve was that right person. Just before Christmas he had asked me if I would like to do an Art Show with him? It was another amazing gesture from an amazing man. I quickly agreed to our combined works being displayed during the annual 2011 NFL Hall of Fame Induction Ceremony. As part of the week-long celebrations, Ed Sabol, Steve's 94-year-old father and the founder of NFL Films, was to be honored. During that August weekend he would be officially enshrined into the NFL Hall of Fame for his lifetime of service and his contributions to the league.

It was an amazing honor for both of the Sabols, as Ed was the first non-football person to be elected into the hall. Senior Mr. Sabol, once an amateur home moviemaker, had never played or coached in the NFL. He was just an ambitious guy with a dream. Fifty years ago, with no professional film experience, "Big Ed" walked into the office of the then NFL Commissioner, Pete Rozelle, and effectively made them an offer they couldn't refuse!

His subsequent life-long efforts helped the league become

the biggest entity in professional sports. Ed Sabol - visionary, dreamer, entertainer and salesman had created NFL Films by simply having the brass balls to speak his mind, follow a dream, and think big!

There's something about this story that sounds hauntingly familiar. I totally understand.

That's where it first occurred to me, in the Canton Ohio Gallery, yes, Steve Sabol and I had been kindred spirits. I said to the crowd, "I met Steve Sabol for the first time, in my imagination, about forty years ago."

Bob's B.S.

"It is simple," I stated. "We are all interested in the people, places and things that are interested in us.

When you begin to notice unexpected events as being synchronized, they cease to be random and start to align themselves. You could say that the "universe" is consciously bringing you the people, places and things that you are unconsciously asking for. All you have to do is notice the random or coincidental experiences and connect the dots (like in a child's coloring book.) Synchronicity starts when you begin to notice what is noticing you," I said to the already engaged audience.

The minute the words came out of my mouth, I knew I would remember and repeat this statement for years to come. At that moment, the audience and I were transported back to 1969. On the field with the Chicago Bears, we shared the visceral feeling of the mud, the blood and the rain.

"In my story, "Finding Your Butkus", I spent 40 years believing that Dick Butkus was my hero," I admitted. "The black, the blue, the white and orange uniforms, and the number

51 all came together for me in this image of a warrior-like, mythic man."

Looking at my painting of "Butkus on the Bench" and his bloody hands, I said, "Do you know who the cameraman was that day in the rain and mud of 1969?"

I paused, looking out into my audience, "Steve Sabol!" I exclaimed. "Do you know who Steve's favorite player of all time was?" I questioned. "That's right! Dick Butkus!"

The resulting gasp and the poetic realization created an "aha" moment for all of us. I continued, "You see, when I wrote to the President of NFL Films and told him my story, I was preaching to the converted! Steve Sabol, through his own passion, had created the image that had haunted me all my life. He was the artist, and the visionary that I had synchronized with since I was a little boy!"

Where alignment may be a subconscious desire, being synchronized is something that, consciously, is hardly even noticed. It seems random in nature.

Unconnected events, people, places and things come into your life at odd times and seemingly without purpose, or so it appears. Looking at it now, every roadblock had created a new beginning.

Whether it was good or bad, I embraced it.

When I finally embraced my life long passion the universe responded with, "Ah finally! We've been waiting for you!"

Bob's B.S.
Every new problem stretched my resolve and had me find a new way to refuse to lose. I kept myself open to the experience - no matter what it brought me.

Years before, as synchronicity would dictate, Steve Sabol had noticed an artistic moment and his moment inspired a lifetime of passion for Bob Mueller.

Between the two, Butkus was right where he was supposed to be – in the middle.

What you are interested in is interested in you.
Synchronicity exists everywhere.
Recall an "Aha" moment in your life or your story and look
for the sychronicitic people, places and things that may have
contributed to it.
Where are you in the story?

Overtime

"Time does not change us. It just unfolds us."
Max Frisch

I wonder if Albert Einstein would approve of the concept of overtime. Is it just me? Or, does the speed of time change near the end of the game, after the two-minute warning? My best guess is that Albert would say, "It is all relative."

The miracle of time is in how we use it. For me it took decades to develop my playbook, but only moments to realize its importance. It's these few relative moments where the magic lies. In the game of life there is no overtime, therefore we must expand time in the places that mean the most to us.

The 2011 Sabol/Mueller Art Show was a minor miracle in itself, as while we were planning the event, Steve became ill and was diagnosed with brain cancer. Though it changed everything for him, he continued to encourage me to make the event happen, and together we found a way.

Like attracts like. Amazingly, Steve was as interested in me as I was in him. The universe had found a way to connect us. The Dallas Cowboy's HOF Quarterback Roger Staubach says, "There are no traffic jams along the extra mile."

It was that extra mile that represented Steve now, as he gave me the opportunity of a lifetime. In turn I walked some of that mile myself by creating an event he was proud to be part of. I don't think I had ever met another man who seemed to have the same sense of rhythm and timing as myself.

I had never really thought of Steve Sabol before, other than as the man who presented shows I liked to watch. It had never occurred to me that these shows were art, his art. He actually wrote, created, and invented an entire style of filmmaking.

I only knew that I liked NFL Football.

Steve Sabol, and his art, had been part of my life for a very long time. I, as a teenager, was an apprentice from afar. It was Steve's stories and sense of art that helped shape me. I had copied them all my life. It's like he had provided the background music to everything I had done.

The synchronicity was that I was unaware I was a part of them. Finding out that I was not separate from the things that I admired was a turning point. I was just as important to them as they were to me. When I made my "self" visible to the world, and began to treat myself as valuable, I aligned with others who shared my passions.

It was hard to believe that I was in Canton Ohio, not just as an observer and a fan, but also, as part of the show. No, it wasn't make-believe.

Bob's B.S.
I was here because of who I am, and because of my desire to listen to voices in my heart, rather than the chatter in my head. .

First, I noticed myself.
Then, I noticed what interested me.
Finally, I noticed what was noticing me.
Sadly, on Tuesday, September 18th, 2012, Steve lost his

battle with cancer. It was about a year after the art show. During that last year, through his assistant Colleen, I had kept a consistent dialogue with him, always hopeful for his recovery.

He called me the day after he received my art book, telling me of the joy it had brought him. "Your stories are wonderful, well written, and well done. Thank you for being my friend," he said. These were his final words to me.

Life is joyful, sometimes bittersweet, and always interesting.

"Tell me a story, and it will live in my heart forever," Steve's mantra rings in my ears.

It turns out, Steve Sabol, the NFL's greatest storyteller, was my true hero. He had given his time to encourage a fellow artist and I am grateful for the special moments he helped to inspire.

One of those inspirations, the movie, "Brian's Song," states, "All true stories end in death, and this is a true story."

Take-away

Accept your own value
and you will recognize your personal power.
Who is your true hero?
Who has been a mentor or inspiration for you?
Who or what are you grateful for?
What actions will you take to reach out and use
the inspiration you have received?

The Extra Point

It's called the conversion. After you score a touchdown you get the opportunity to kick for an "extra point." Even though you have scored a touchdown, you still need to convert what you have done to get the point!

Today, you are the sum total of your experiences. You are uniquely qualified to take what you know, and make it mean something.

If you are like me, you have probably had both successes and failures throughout your life. Does it matter whether you scored or were scored upon? I think not. It only matters that you convert your experience, and get the extra point. It's what you make it mean.

"Being challenged in life is inevitable. Being defeated is optional." - Roger Crawford

The question is, what will you do next? When you look at your stories, do you see the lessons? If the answer is yes; you are ready to formulate your playbook.

As I said in the beginning, finding something assumes that you are looking for it! I guarantee that whatever you decide to look for, you will find. Remember, life is a game, and the game is meant to be played. You gotta play all four quarters, take the good with the bad, and learn from it all. Take your stories, as they are the tools of your experiences, and then take a shot.

Or to quote "the great one", Wayne Gretzky,

"You miss 100% of the shots you don't take!"

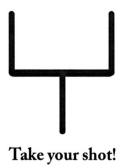

Take your shot!

MORE PRAISE FOR FINDING YOUR BUTKUS

"In martial arts we have katas, in football we have plays and in life we have a game plan. Mueller has somehow combined all three into this fantastic must read book that will lead you down the road of success."
Don Warrener, Warrener Entertainment

"Bob Mueller reminded me of the personal power we all have inside, he continually inspires and motivates me as an Artist"
Brandon Whitehead, Illustrator Chicago IL

"The work that lays before you, 'Finding Your Butkus – The Four Quarters,' by Emmy recipient, Bob Mueller, is filled with so much 'BS!' In spite of thousands of self-help books having been written over the years, none combine an NFL Playbook, the Law of Attraction and Conceptual Philosophy of the Warrior Arts... it is totally unique. The author's 'BS,' [Belief Systems], represents a fresh look at how to turn dreams into realities. It's a story with guts ... 'Persistence meets the Law of Attraction.' I simply couldn't put it down, it was like discovering for the first time that I am the person sent to save me. Mueller's BS is an amazing story with a great Kickoff and fantastic 4th Quarter comeback. It's good old fashioned innocence, ambition and Dick Butkus' old school values about how to be a winner in life."
Patrick McCarthy, PHD 9th Dan Hanshi

"Rather than a handbook, it's a playbook full of motivational messages that combine to support you in making your Heaven on Earth real!"
Martin Rutte Co-author, *Chicken Soup for the Soul at Work*

"Finding Your Butkus goes beyond the thousands of self-help books saying the same thing. What he brings is something fresh and full of Bob's B.S. (Belief Systems)"
Barb Reese

"After nearly a lifetime of martial arts successes, award winning artistic pursuits and passion for all things sports related, Bob Mueller steps into a new arena. His new offering 'Finding Your Butkus: The Four Quarters,' is a no nonsense experience based guidebook to personal success. The work is an amalgam of meeting notable greats from varied fields, and breaking down their unique philosophies into practical, highly useful chapters. A must text for a jolt of mental motivation."
Cezar Borkowski, Founder NKS
Technical Direction Canadian Black Belt HOF

"I picked this book up not knowing how game plays from 'THE' American icon sport NFL could have much meaning to an Aussie? How wrong I was! Having already achieved most things in my chosen fields - now I want to go out and achieve them all over again with a new found enthusiasm !!! A motivational book that's be hard to put down."
Andrew Kennedy, Grafx inc. Australia

"From the Artist's Statement to the Extra Point ... Finding Your Butkus scores", Mueller's lessons about the importance of heroes is timely."
Sam Moledzki, 8th dan President, Karatedo Shitokai

"Bob Mueller clearly demonstrates why heroes are indeed valuable and especially so needed now."
Bob Salomon, Best Selling Author

"Good old fashioned, old school values about how to be a winner in life."
John Therrien, President World Kobudo Federation

"I was drawn to a particular chapter in your book, 'A true playbook on how to get what you want'. For me to truly get what I want wanted, I implemented my 3 P's. Planning- Know what you want to devise a plan on how to get it. Make sure your plan is sound and that you have a way to overcome most hurdles that can arise. Patience- Anything worth having is worth working for. And its virtually impossible to sustain long-term, worth-wild success if you're immediately rewarded with un-earned success (lottery winners). Perseverance- There will most definitely be hurdles to overcome, (didn't get the job at first, didn't get that bonus or loan I thought I would, so on) but you have to focused on your goal. Learn from your mistakes and try to prevent them from happening again. and just when you think it's time to give up on your dream, refer back to the first 2 principles and push forward. There will be gold at the end of your rainbow."
Lincoln Kennedy, Oakland Raiders Ret

"Bob Mueller has a knack for helping others, through his books. He will touch everyone with a compatible life interest. I believe that after going through every line in this book, your life's journey may never be the same. We have been good friends for decades now and whether it's his paintings that hang on my walls, his martial arts or just listening to his motivational speeches, Finding Your Butkus will inspire you to find your full potential."
Professor Don Jacob, H.B.Mg, Founder of Purple Dragon International Karate, Author of *The Fighting Man's Bible*

During my 40 year journey as an artist, I have encountered situations where questions would arise along the lines of, "what would my peers think?", or "I wonder if the public will get the wrong impression of me". Creatives must learn to allow themselves to be who they dream and to proceed without superficial boundaries. Only then can one realize all of their potentials. I discovered that when others began to embrace my "oddities", good karma and success ensued. Bob's book takes a new and unique look and life's challenges and puts them into real-life situations. His examples, though many sports-related, are really parables that can be used in any situation. I am confident that reading this book will take your dreams into reality."
Randall Hedden, Artist

Mueller's 'W.O.W. formula" and 'The Dive Play' are unique, insightful and motivating tools that apply to my life right now! Working your "Inner Butkus" is profound - I believe his message will be motivationally speaking to the masses. Tony Robbins move over, Big Bobby Mueller is in the house!"
Rory Millikin, CEO, and international award winning inventor

"It's not what you did, it's what you do next that counts!" A compelling read. Combining lessons from a lifetime of martial arts, the grit of the grid-iron and strong self-belief Mueller paints an inspirational road map to help you navigate and succeed in the playing field of life!"
Erik Y. Magraken, Partner MacIsaac & Company Injury Lawyers

Author Biography

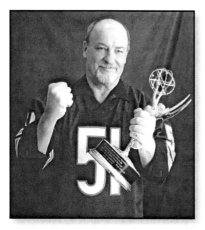

Born in Winnipeg, Manitoba, as the son of a military officer he moved endlessly, but his formative years were spent on the Esquimalt naval base in Victoria BC. No one knows why he was attracted to football as no one in his family liked sports. With only one black & white TV in the home and no one else interested in watching sports, it remains a family mystery. Yet at the age of nine or ten Bob loved football. Leaving home at 16 years old he had major careers as a carpenter/builder, a karate teacher/martial arts entrepreneur, a hot yoga teacher/studio owner and as an internationally recognized sports artist.

He coined the term "Transition Warrior" for his ability to embrace change and to thrive on the unexpected. Bob is constantly working to the edge of his talent, always creative: creating art, writing, short films and always talking, teaching and wondering what's next?

More About Bob Mueller

Bob Mueller is a motivating speaker with a unique story. He inspires confidence, courage and hope in others from a lifetime of leadership and teaching.

He combines his incredible life's journey and its lessons to create a PLAYBOOK for SUCCESS. Mueller speaks to companies, groups and events.

What could you and your company learn about focus, self-motivation, leadership, and commitment to your goals from a 7th Degree Black Belt, Emmy Winning Artist?

What happens when you start to listen and you begin to follow your inner talents and desires?
They come true!

www.findingyourbutkus.com
findingyourbutkus@mail.com

CPSIA information can be obtained
at www.ICGtesting.com
Printed in the USA
LVOW10s1216291217
561199LV00007B/18/P